BEHIND MOUNTAINS

KEHRER

BEHIND MOUNTAINS

RAGNAR AXELSSON

Time has a way of offering new perspectives on life and what has passed. Reviewing the photographs from past roundups in Landmannaafréttur reminds me of this. They stir up deep emotions over how magnificent the life of sheep farmers there has been through the years. These images have stayed with me long after they were taken, capturing moments that have really never left my mind.

It is a bittersweet feeling standing on a mountaintop, gazing out over stunning views of mountains, canyons, and valleys, recalling moments that will never return. There is longing but also gratitude for having spent time in this majestic landscape shaped by volcanoes and unforgiving elements, among the people whose lives in these mountains have shaped the land's character, and who I consider lifelong friends. If I close my eyes, I can hear in the wind the imagined shouts and calls of the herders, the clatter of horses' hooves, and the bleating of sheep. They are all heading home, just before winter blankets the mountains in white.

Even in the rugged environment of Landmannaafréttur, the balance between man and nature is a delicate one. Mountain herding relies on specific knowledge, passed down through generations, that emphasises community, organisation, and endurance. But time brings change. In culture, technology, and the environment itself. What will the future of the mountain roundups be? Will the people who depend on, protect, and care for their land be able to continue in their ways? Can the freedom of the mountains remain undisturbed? What is to come is uncertain. But as Þórður Guðnason, a man of these mountains and my guide through them, says, 'no matter what happens, the mountains will remain in their place'.

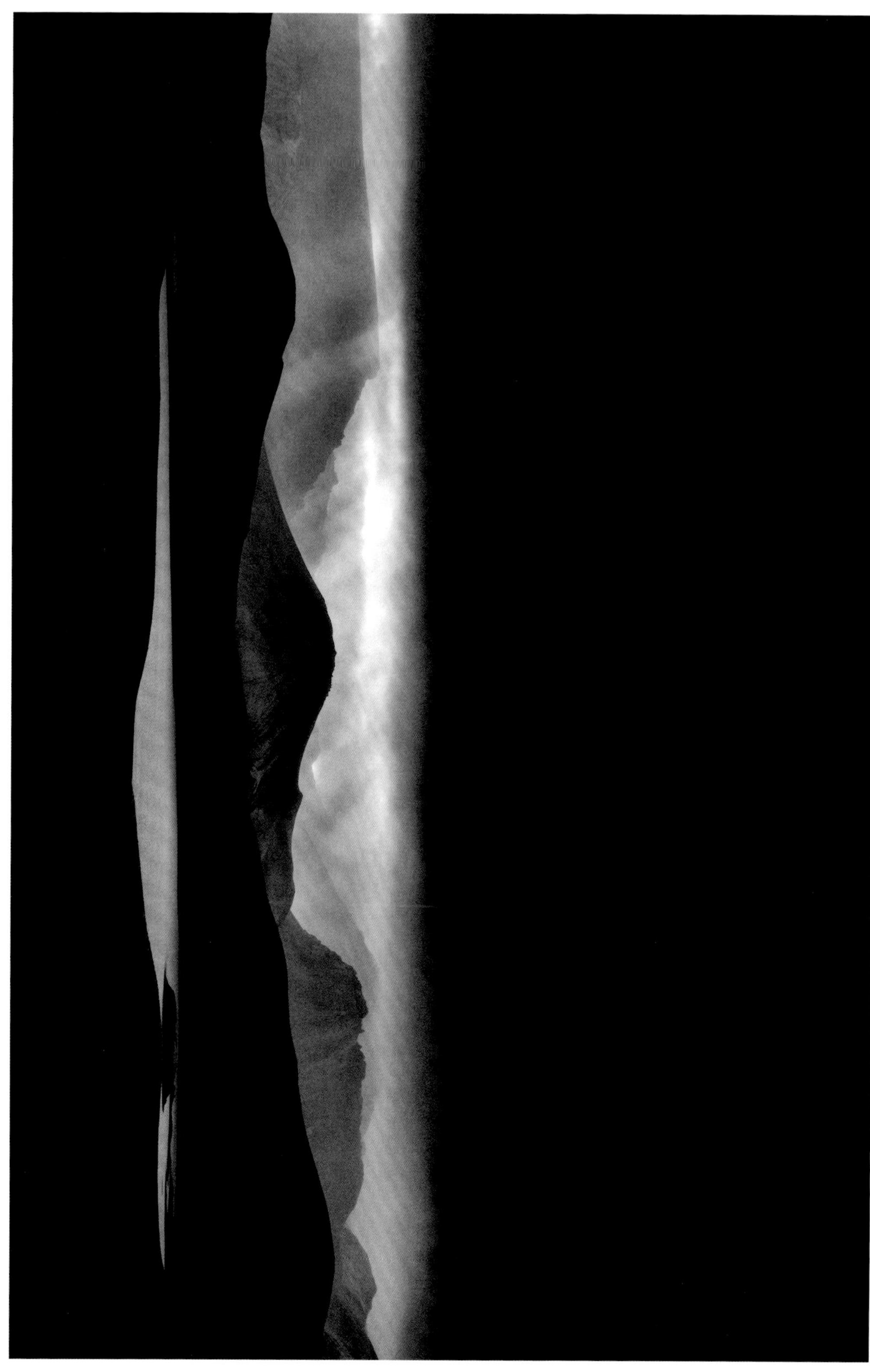

Landmannaafréttur is a remote, highland region in the southern interior of Iceland. It stretches from the volcano Hekla in the west, to the glacial area Jökulheimar to the east, and lies both in an active volcanic zone and on a rift between the North American and Eurasian tectonic plates. It is a powerful geologic area containing three volcanic systems (Hekla, Torfajökull, and the Veiðivötn lakes), as well as Landmannalaugar, the country's most expansive geothermal area.

Hidden behind mountains, Landmannaafréttur is an area of astonishing, almost otherworldly, colour and form. While most of Iceland is made up of dark basalt, the pale rhyolite stone of the massive Torfajökull volcanic crater at the region's centre gives it its striking character. Sunlight glows luminescent in its ridges and gorges. And over millennia, geothermal heat, glacial erosion, and harsh weather have turned the bare stone hills and valleys a spectrum of uncanny shades of copper, red, green, and turquoise. Underfoot there are fields of glassy obsidian, tracts of black sand, icy glaciers, and lush, mossy slopes. And all around, signs of magma underground is still in the process of transforming the surface: bubbling grey mud pots stinking of sulphur; gaping, steaming fumaroles; cloudy blue geothermal ponds; and other clear mineral waters, both warm and cold, to bathe in.

Every autumn, the sheep farmers of Landmannaafréttur journey into this area to round up their animals from summer pastures. Following ancient traditions of communal herding, they spend a week in September's wildly shifting weather, searching for, gathering, and driving the sheep down the mountains into a great, circular collecting pen for sorting back to their respective farms. Largely unchanged for centuries, this arduous task is still primarily conducted on horseback or on foot, across some of the most challenging and breathtaking terrain in Iceland.

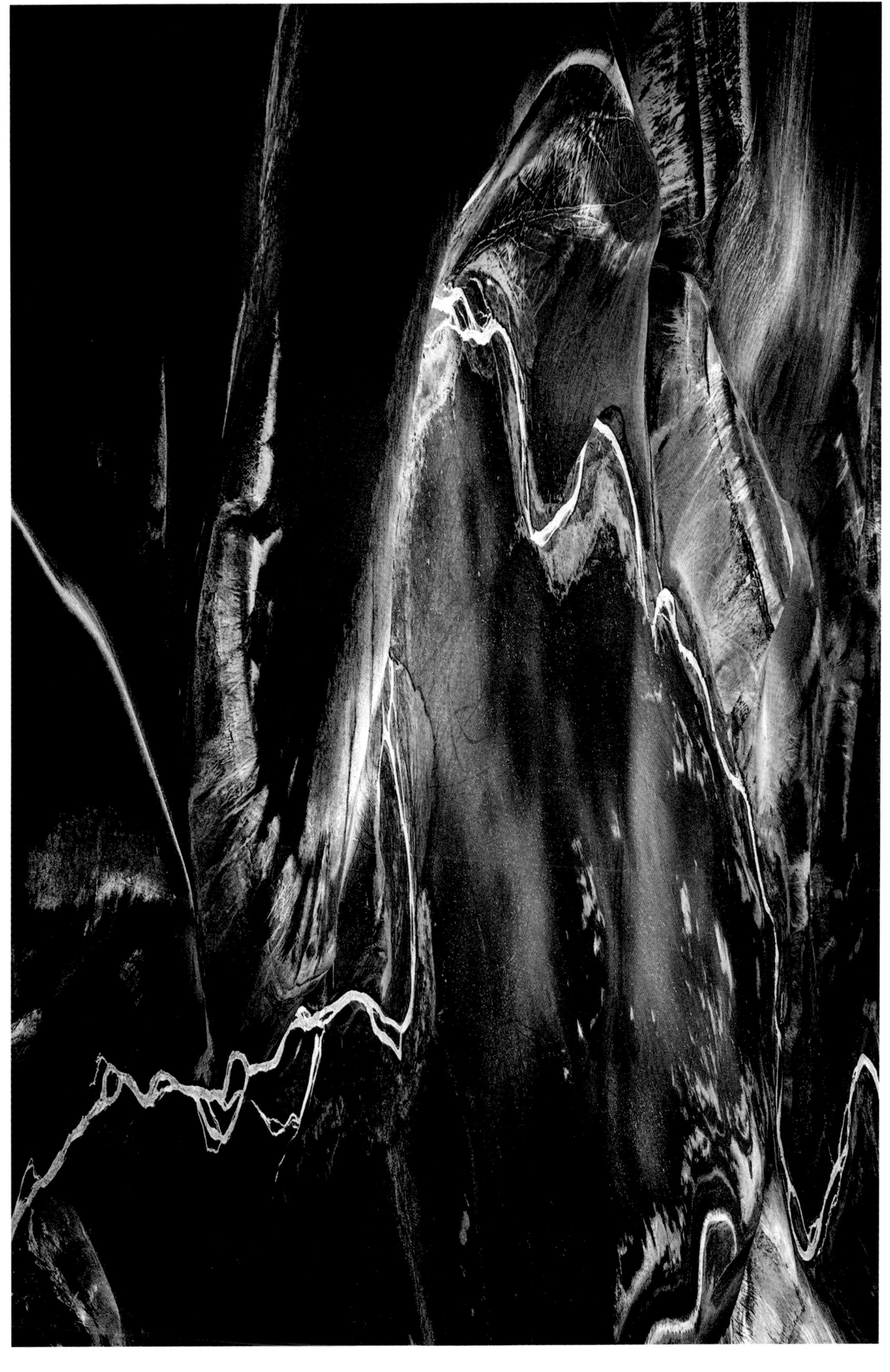

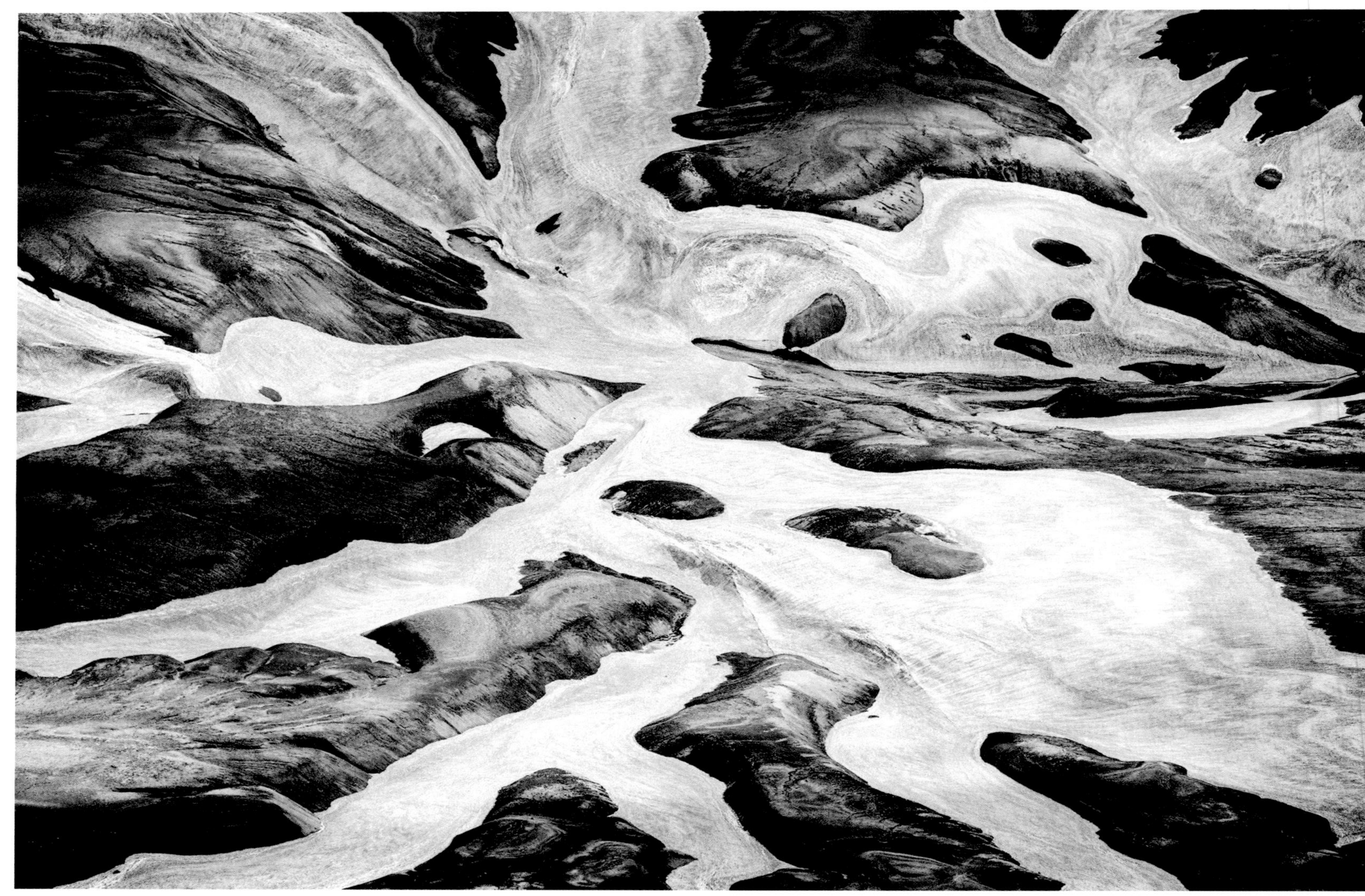

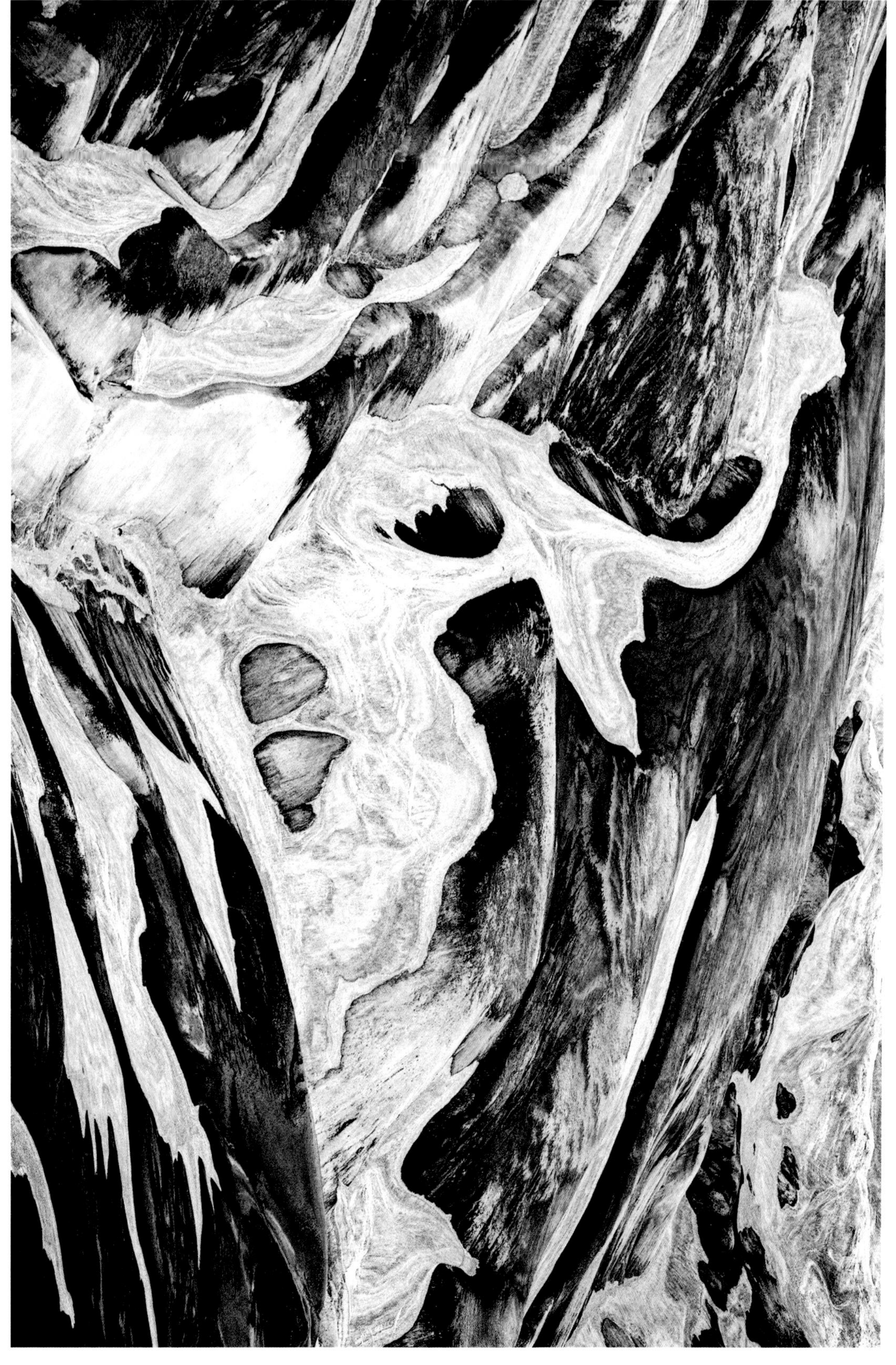

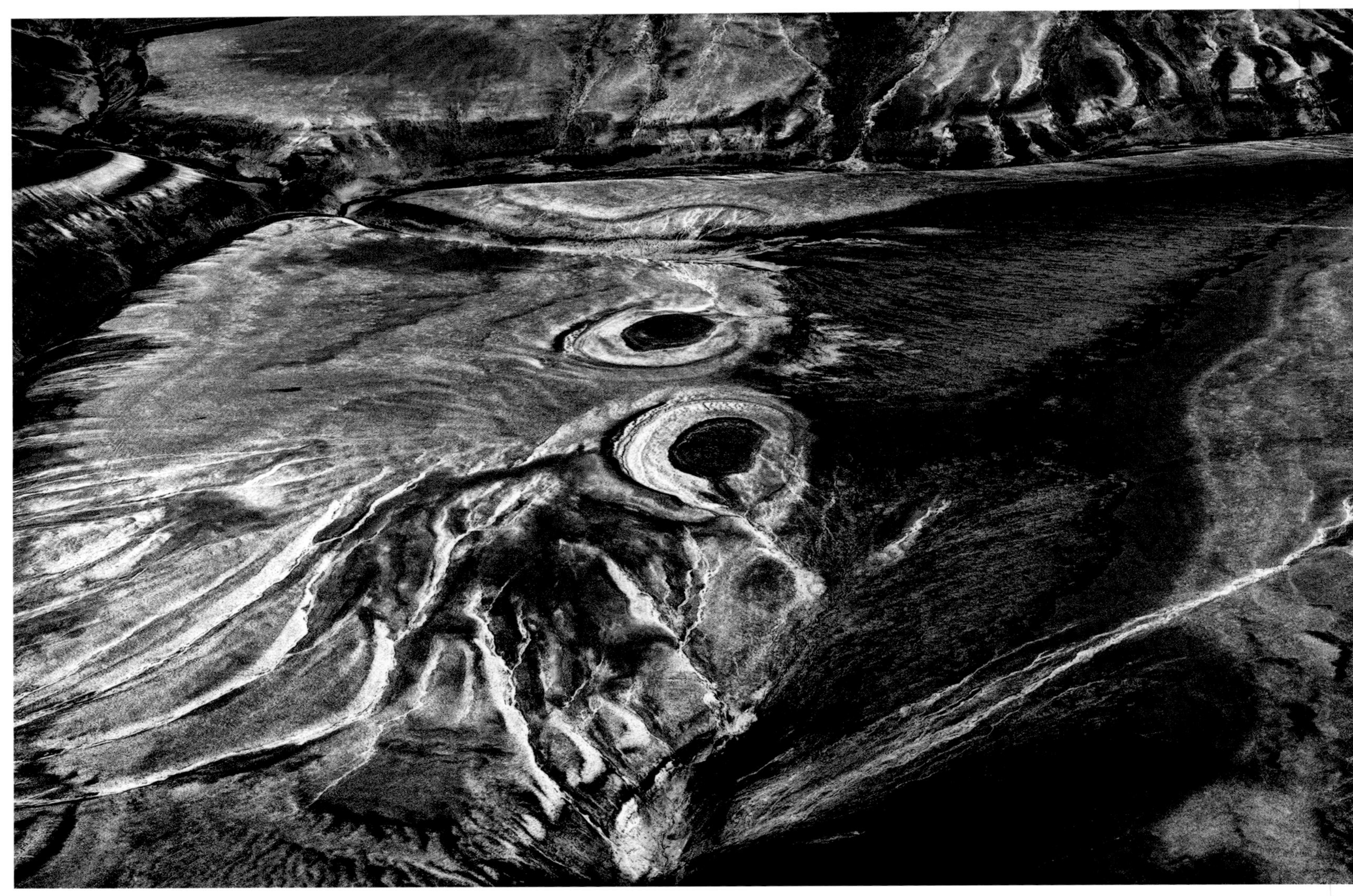

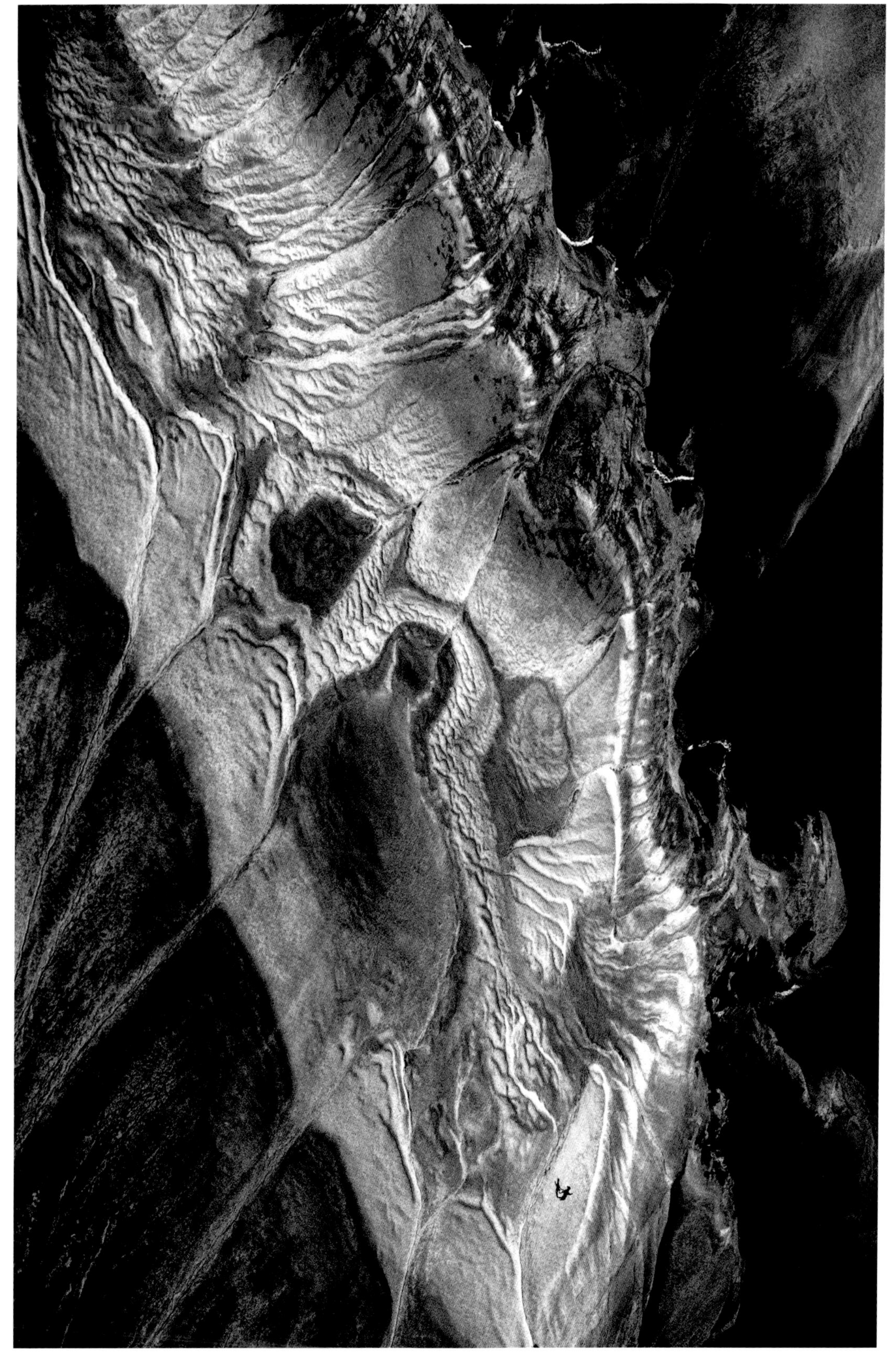

I

Dawn

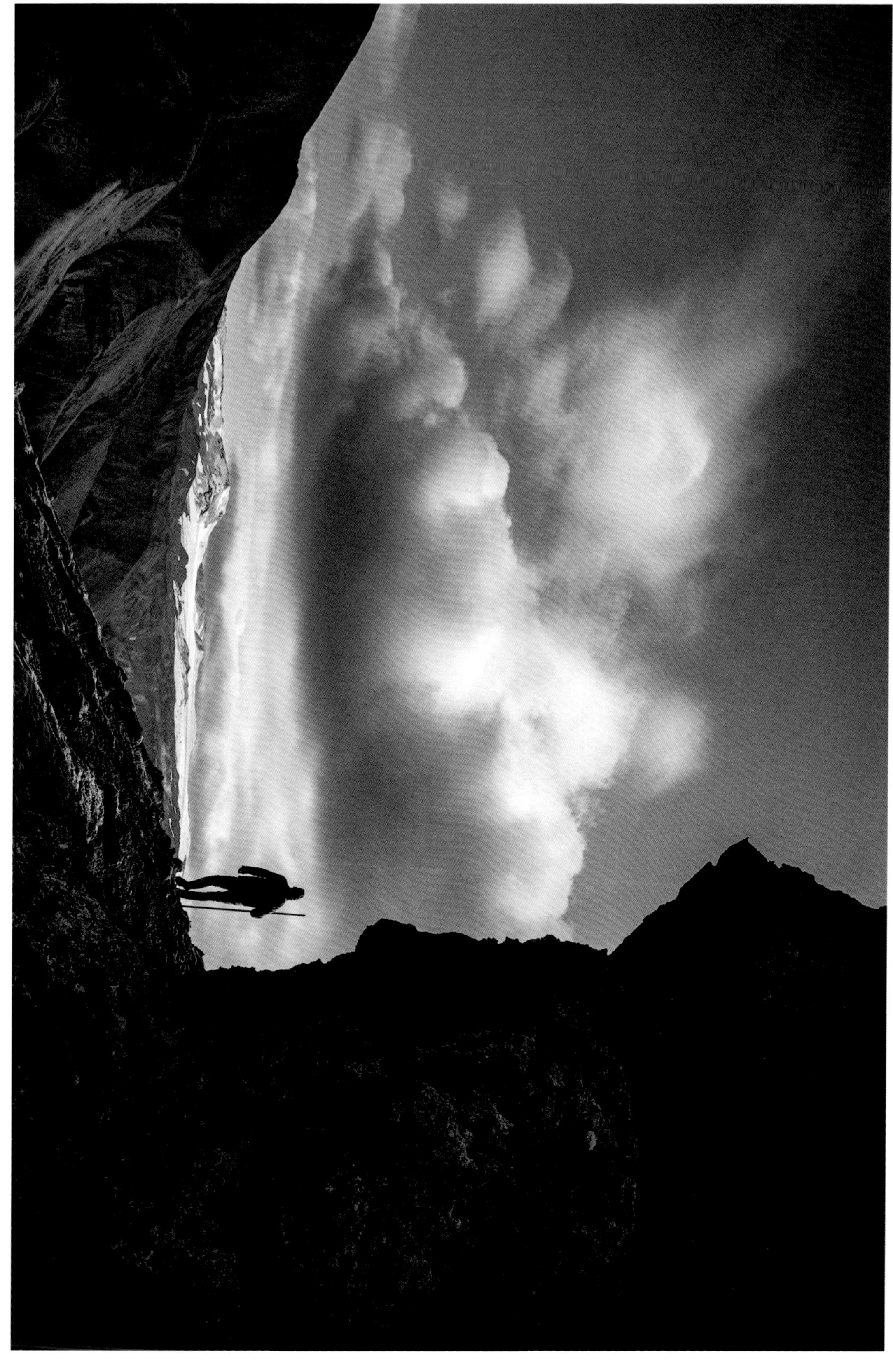

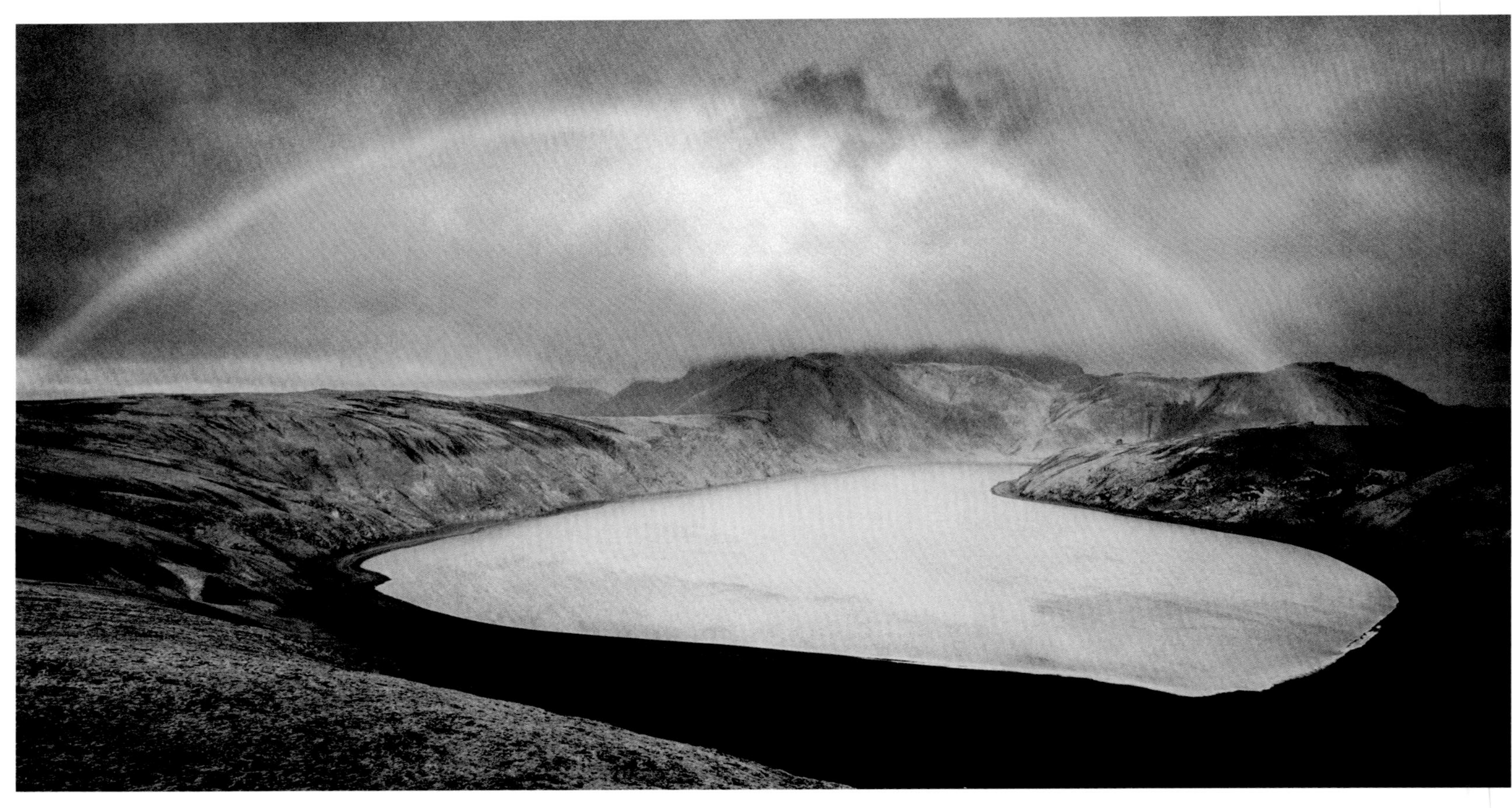

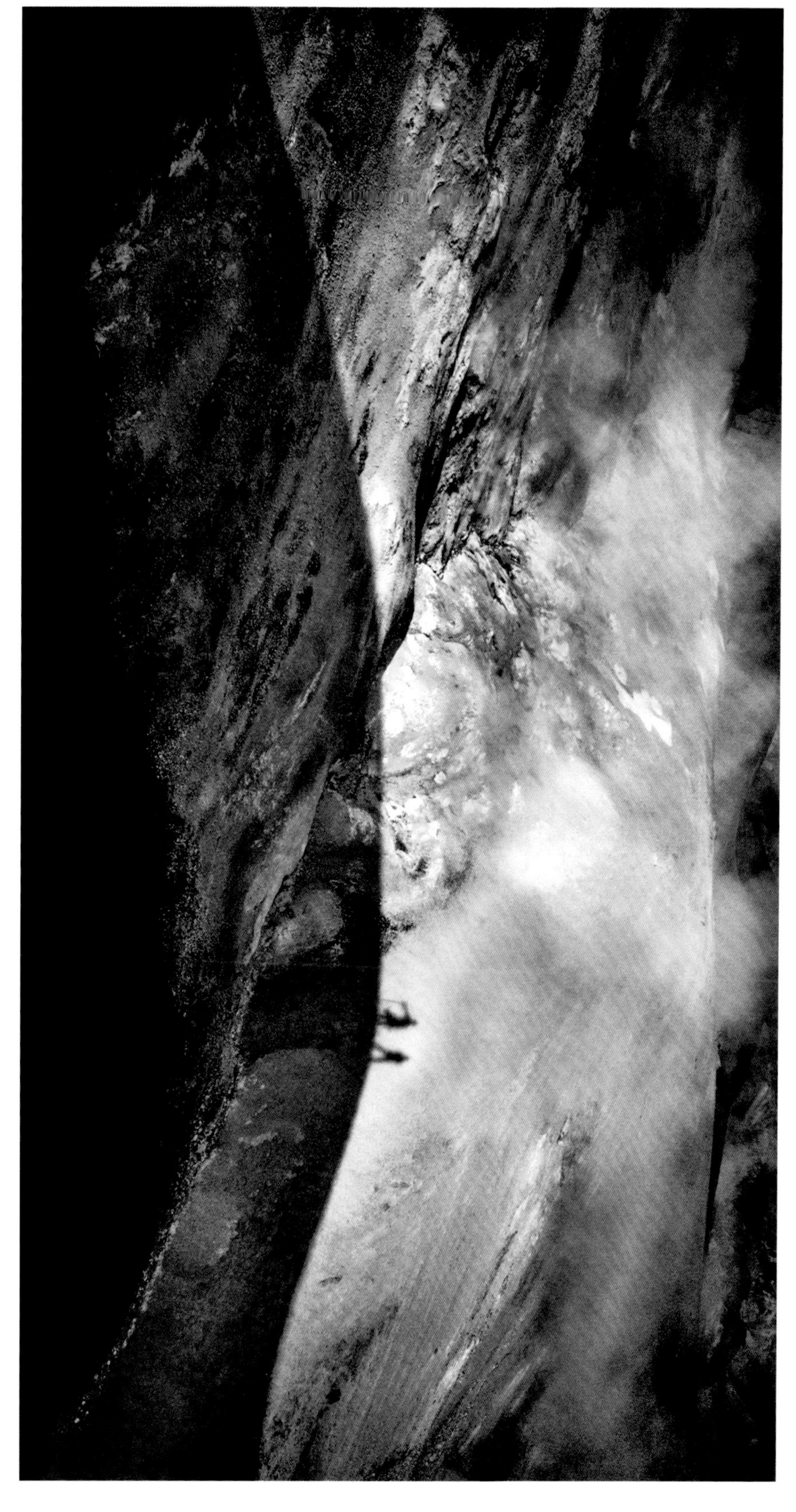

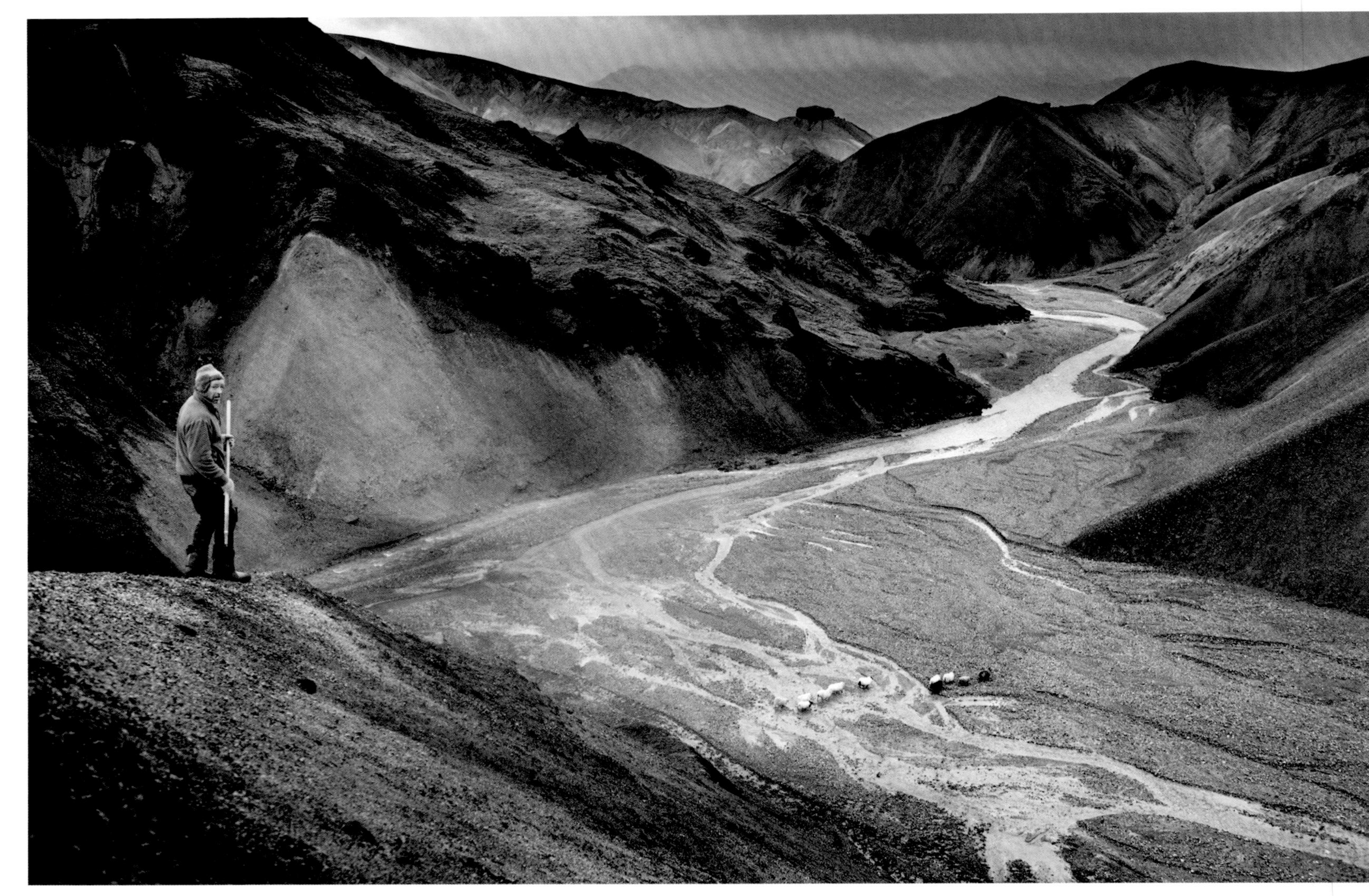

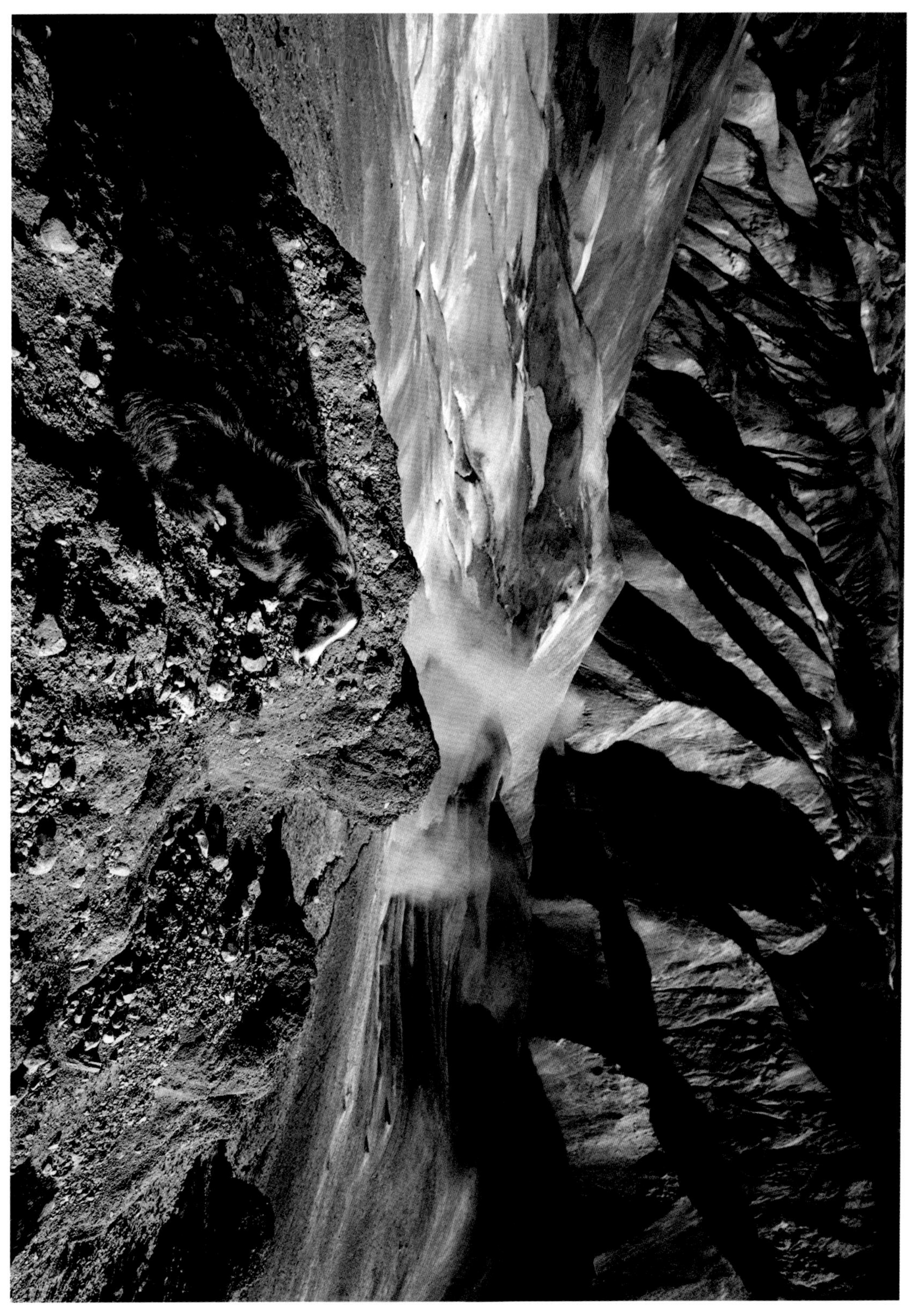

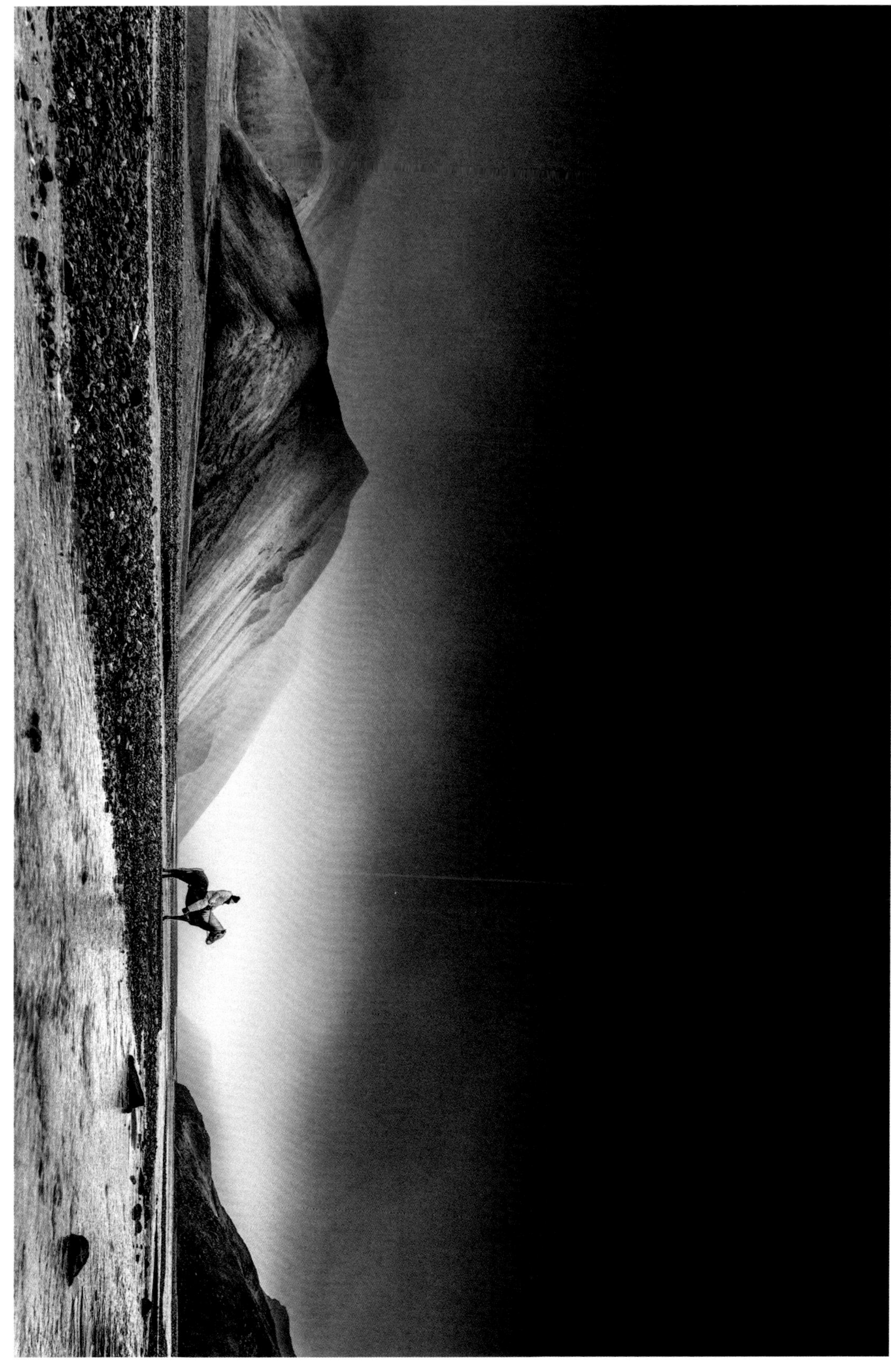

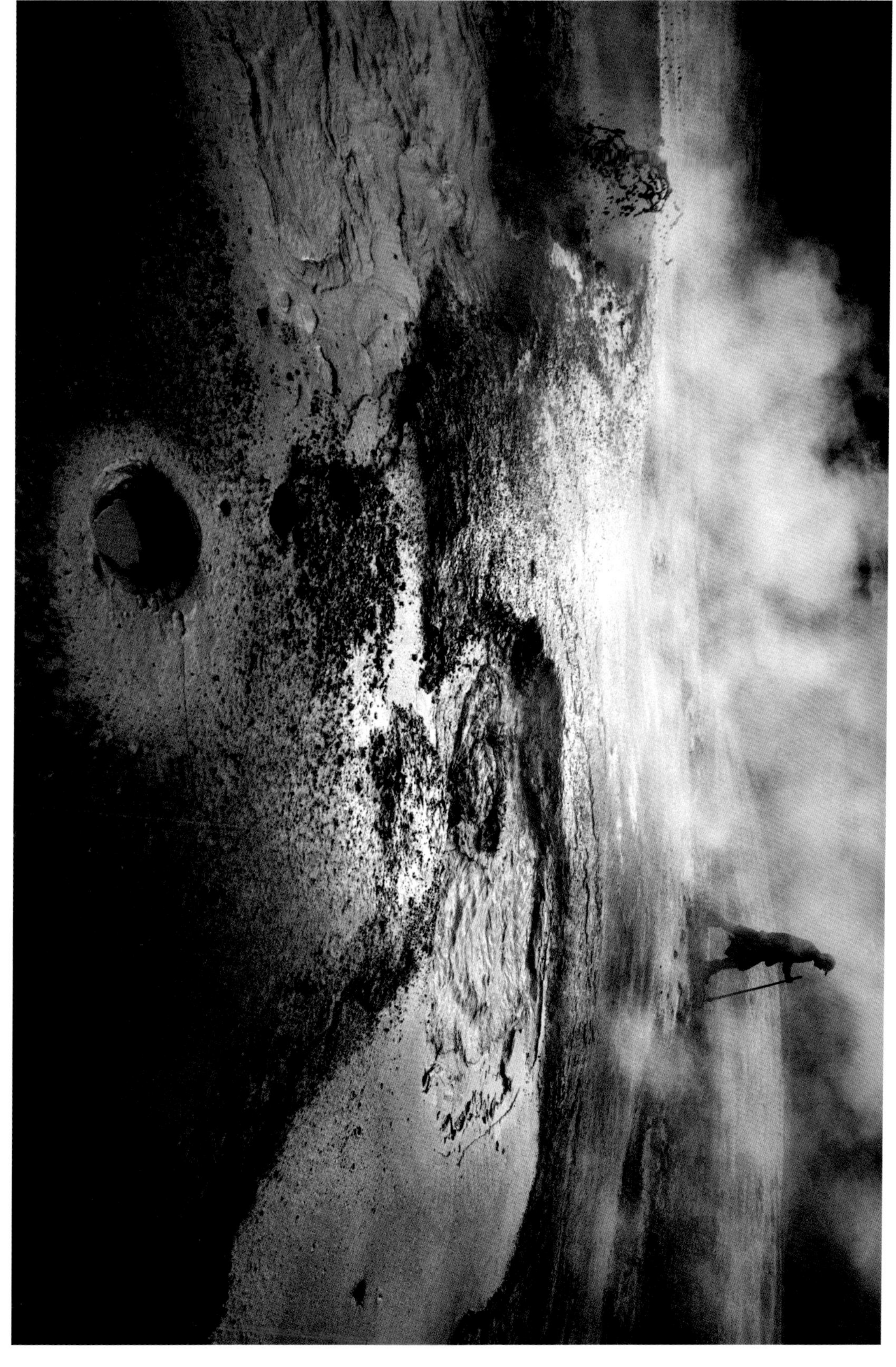

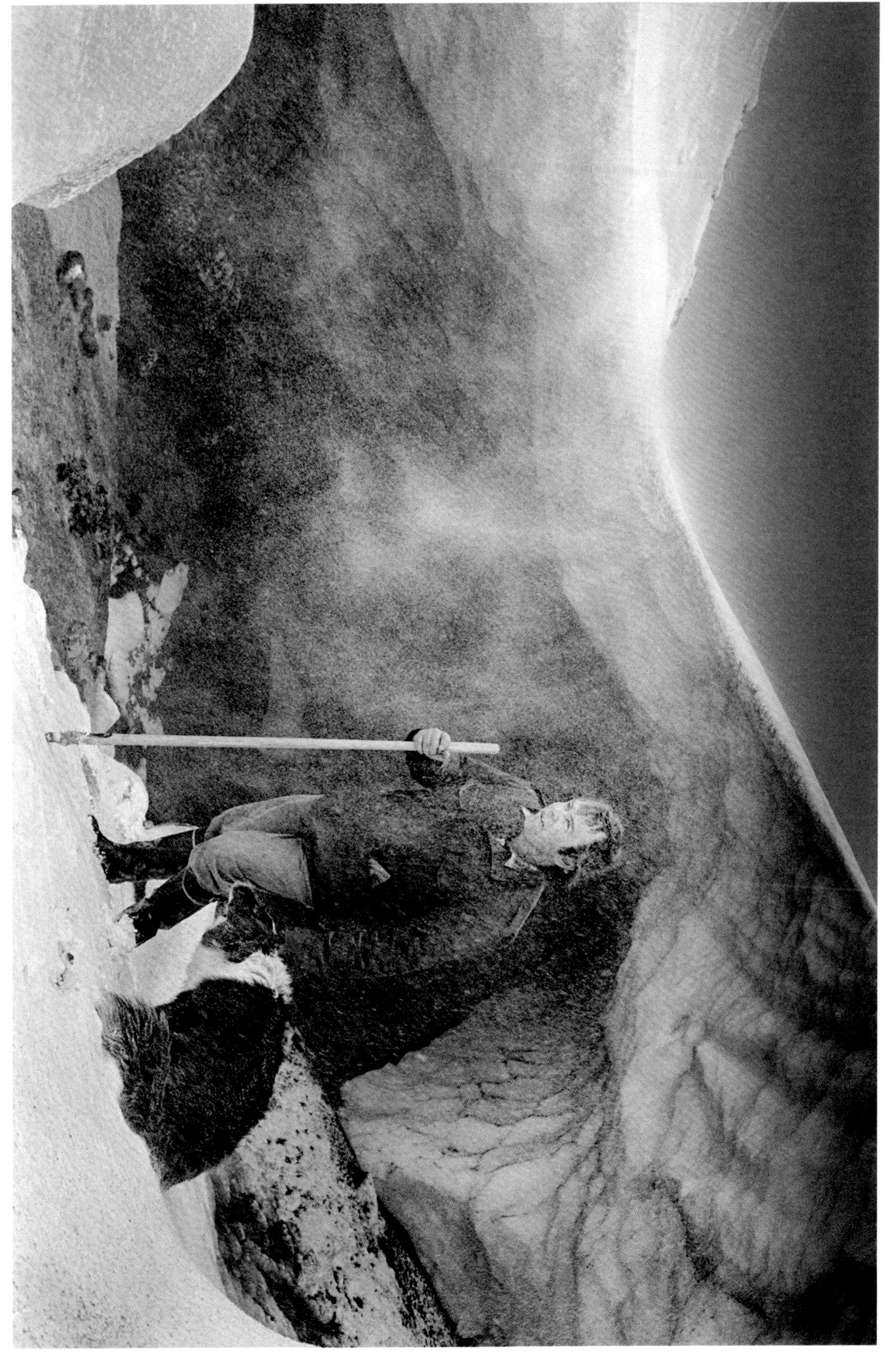

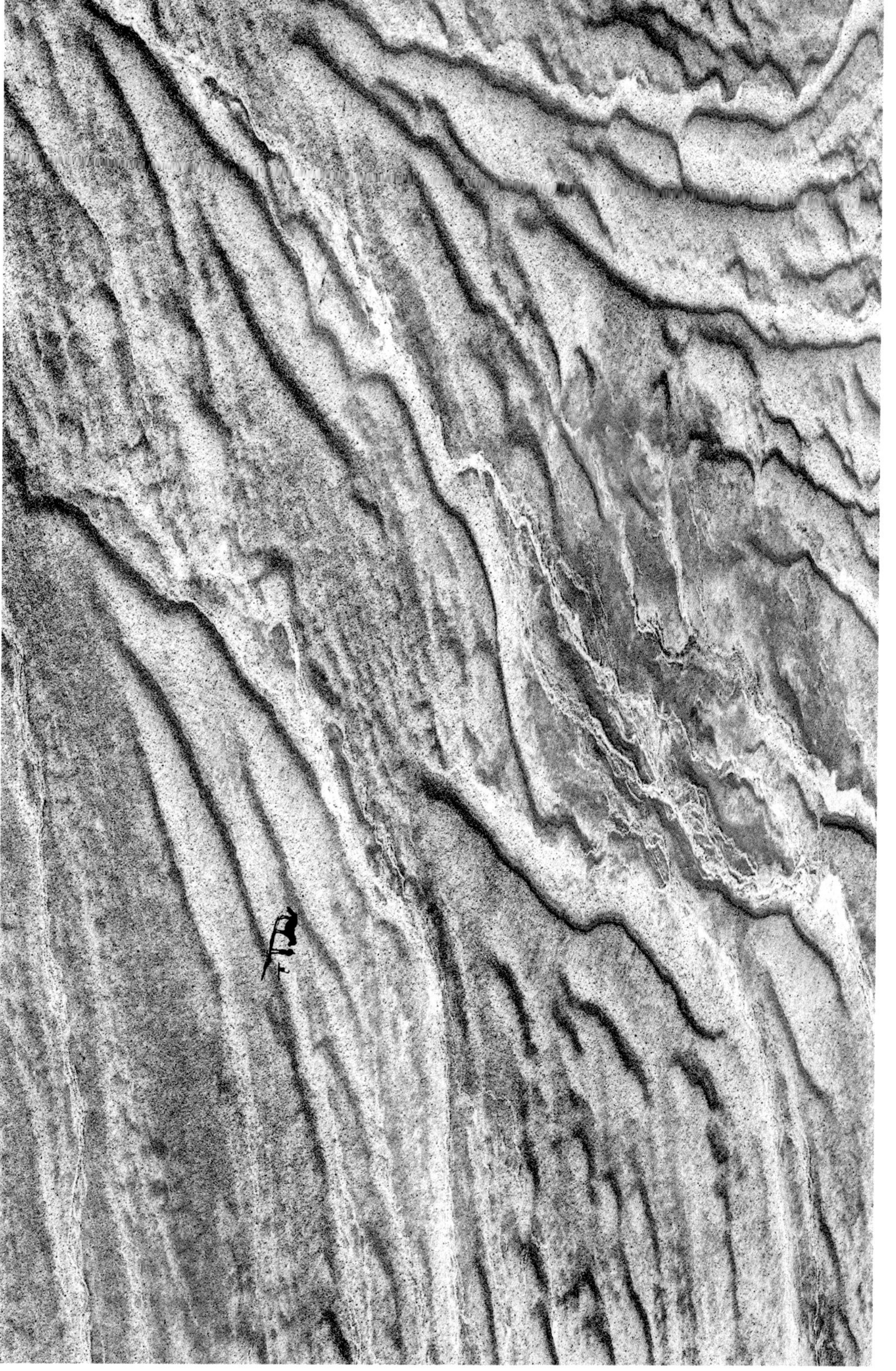

II

Gathering

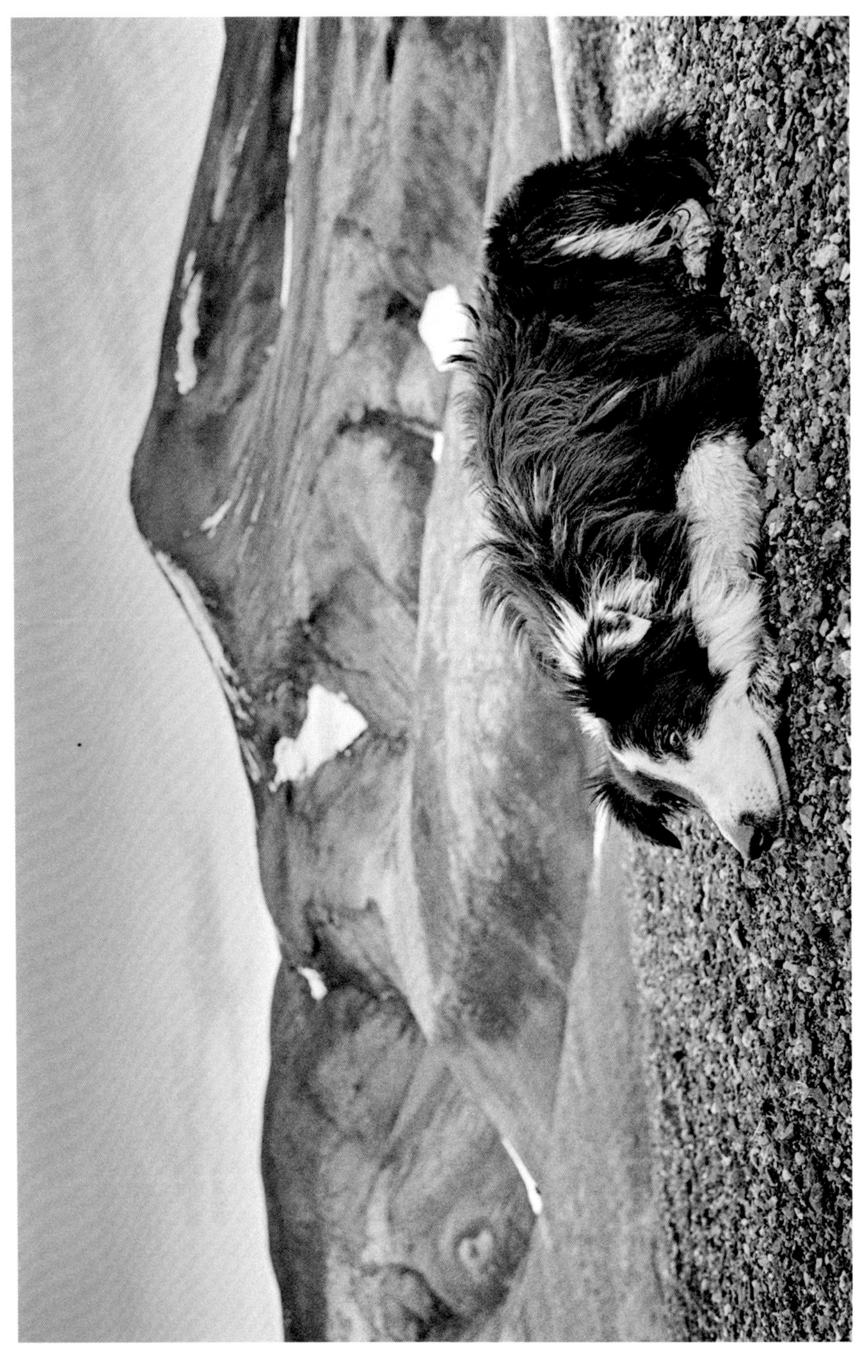

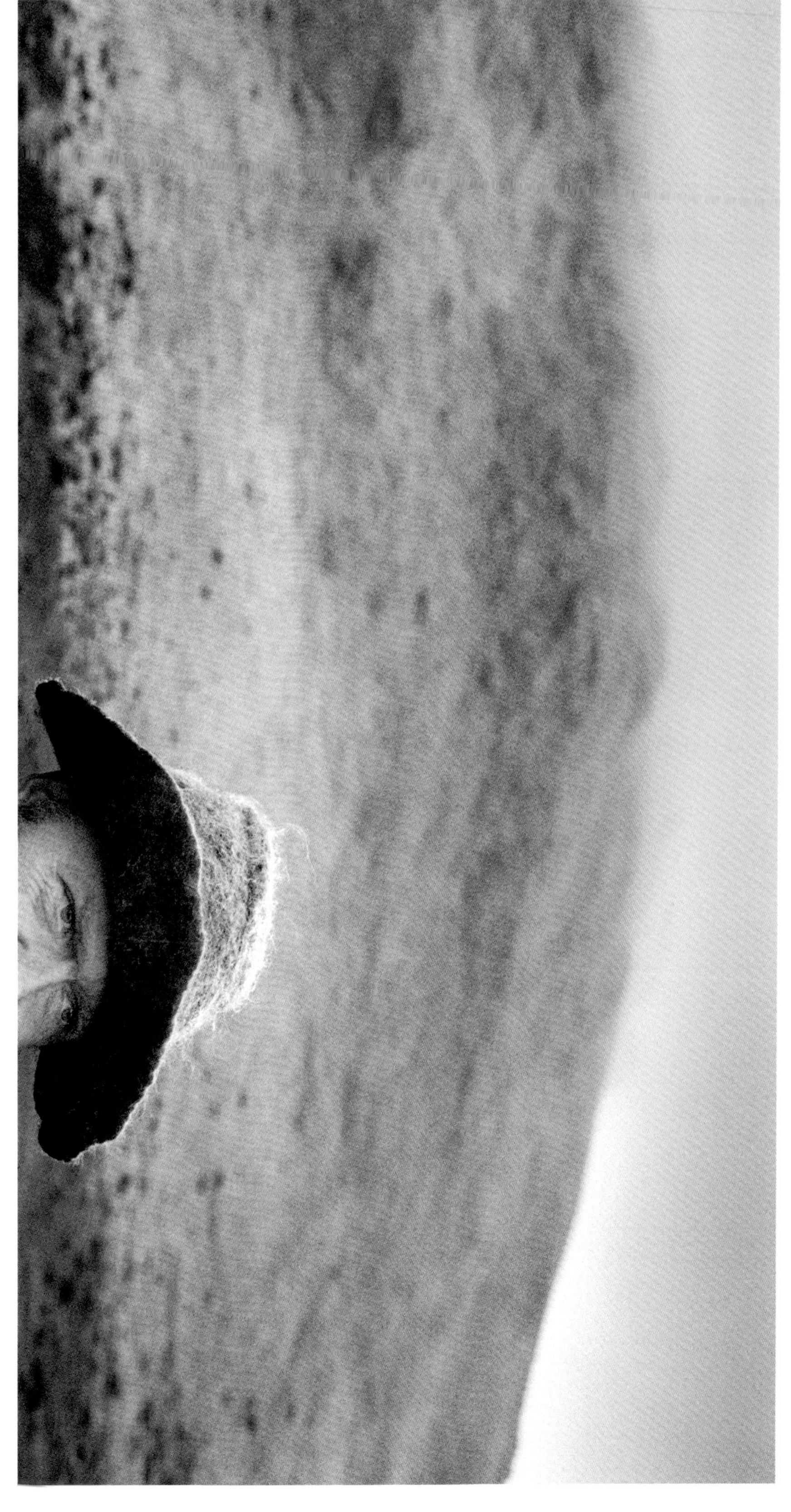

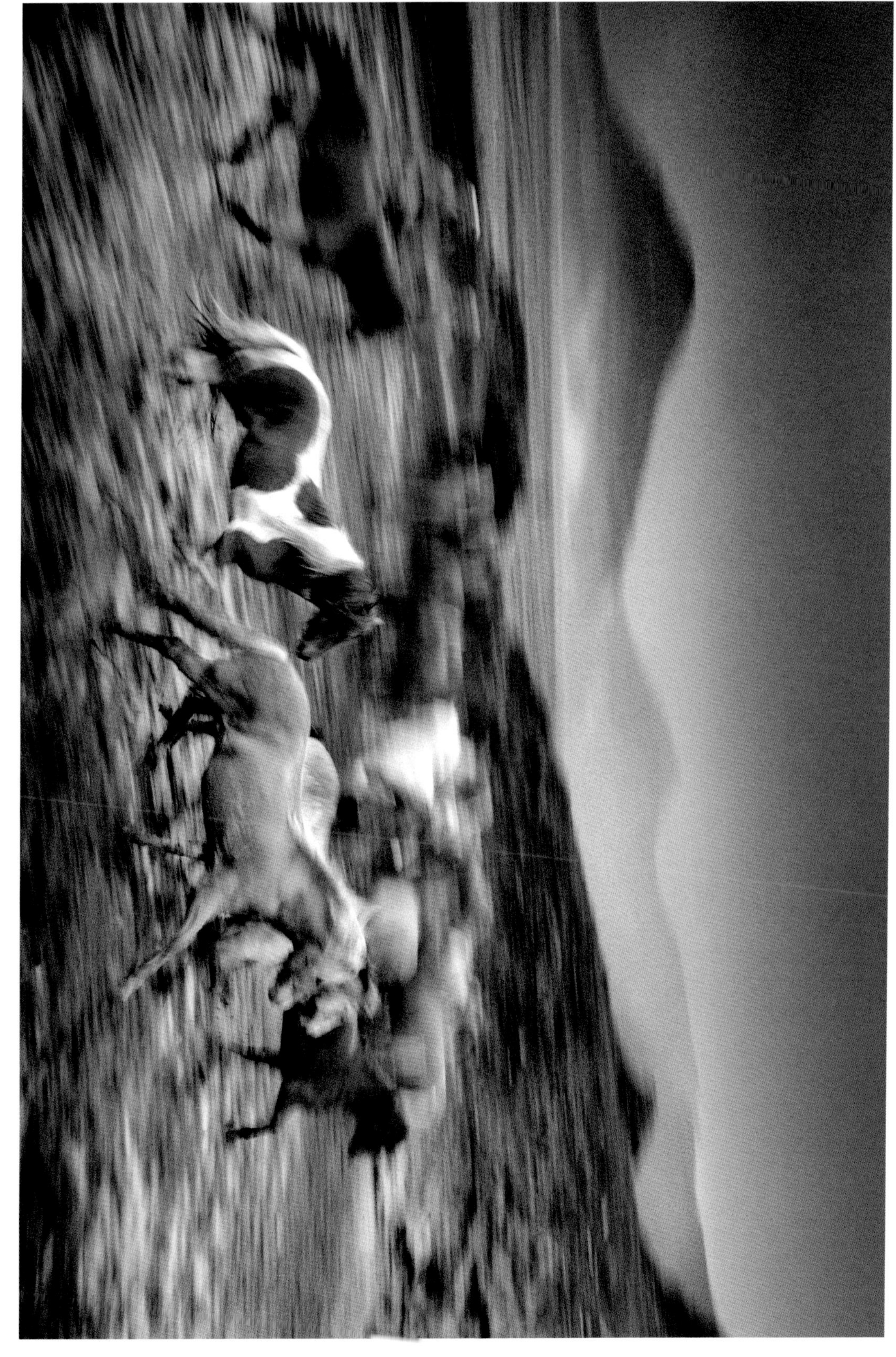

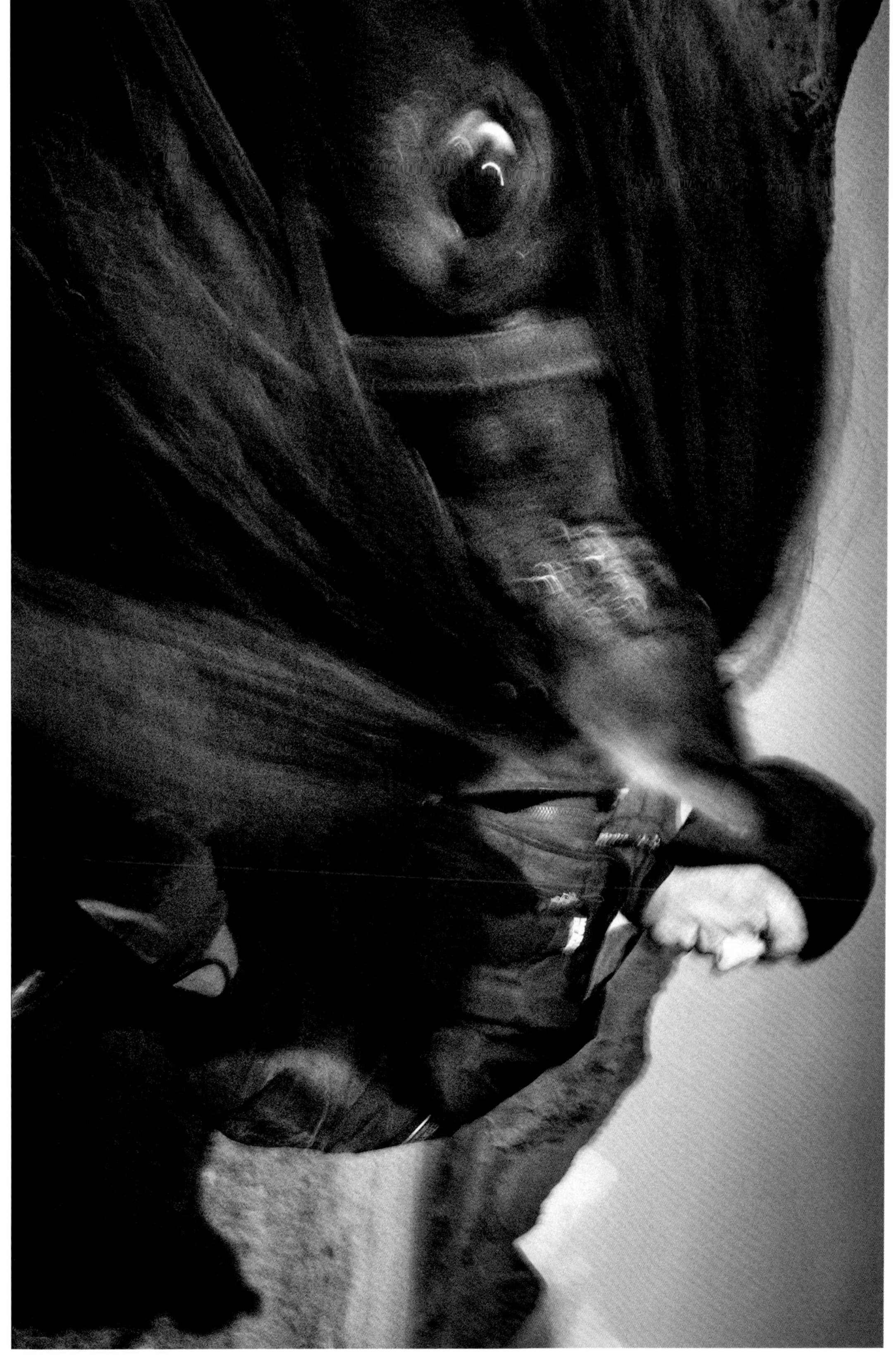

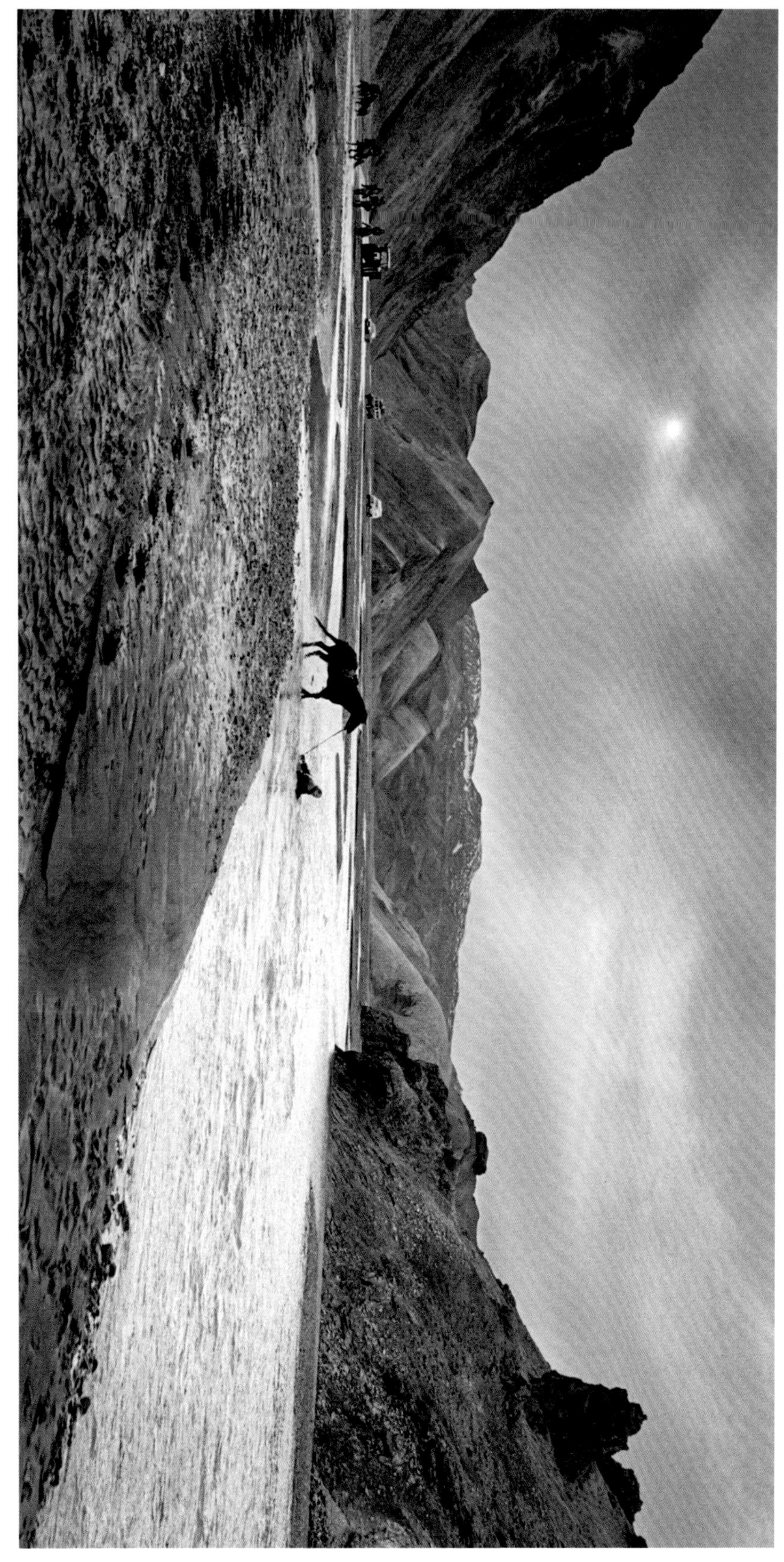

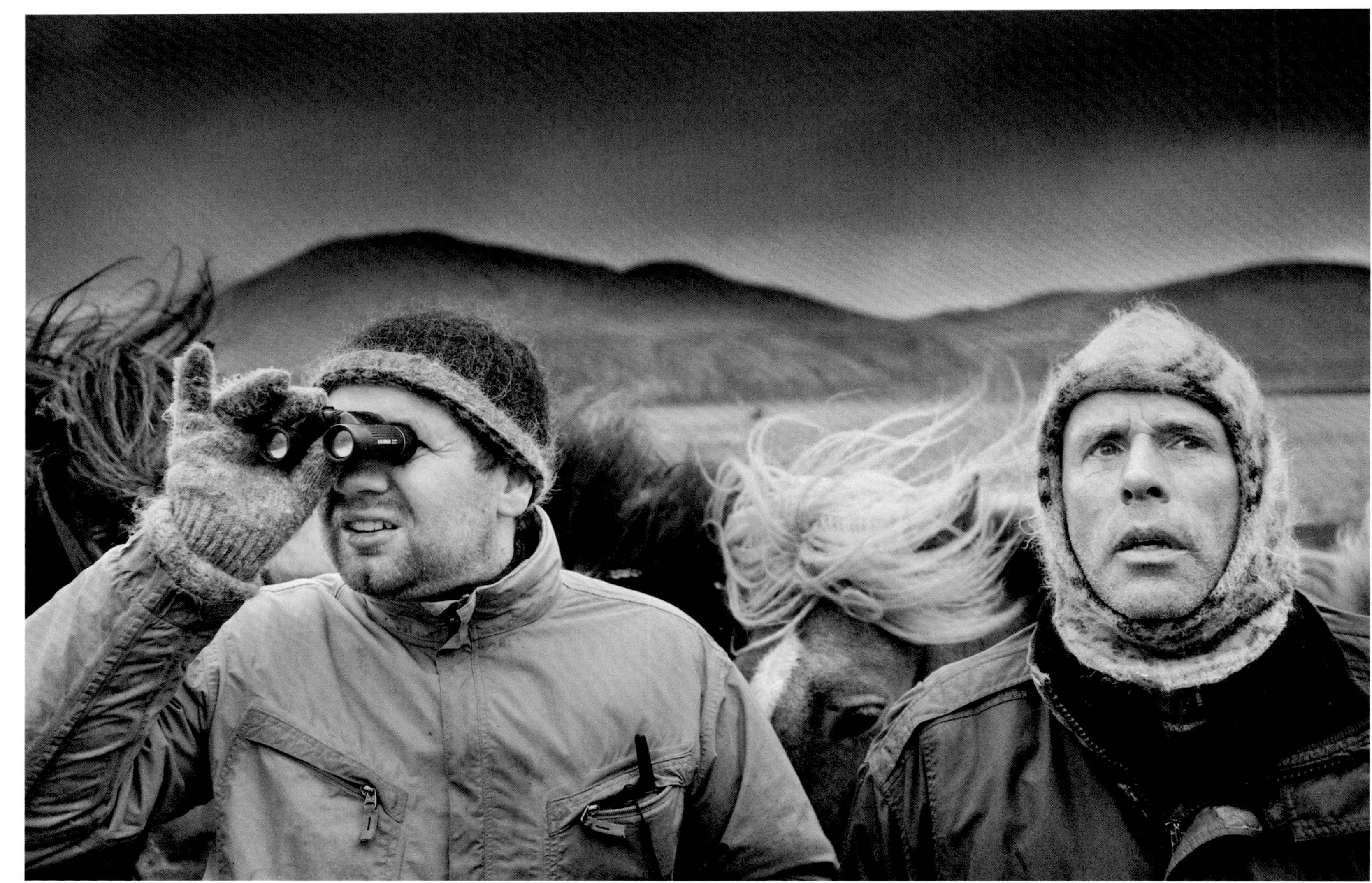

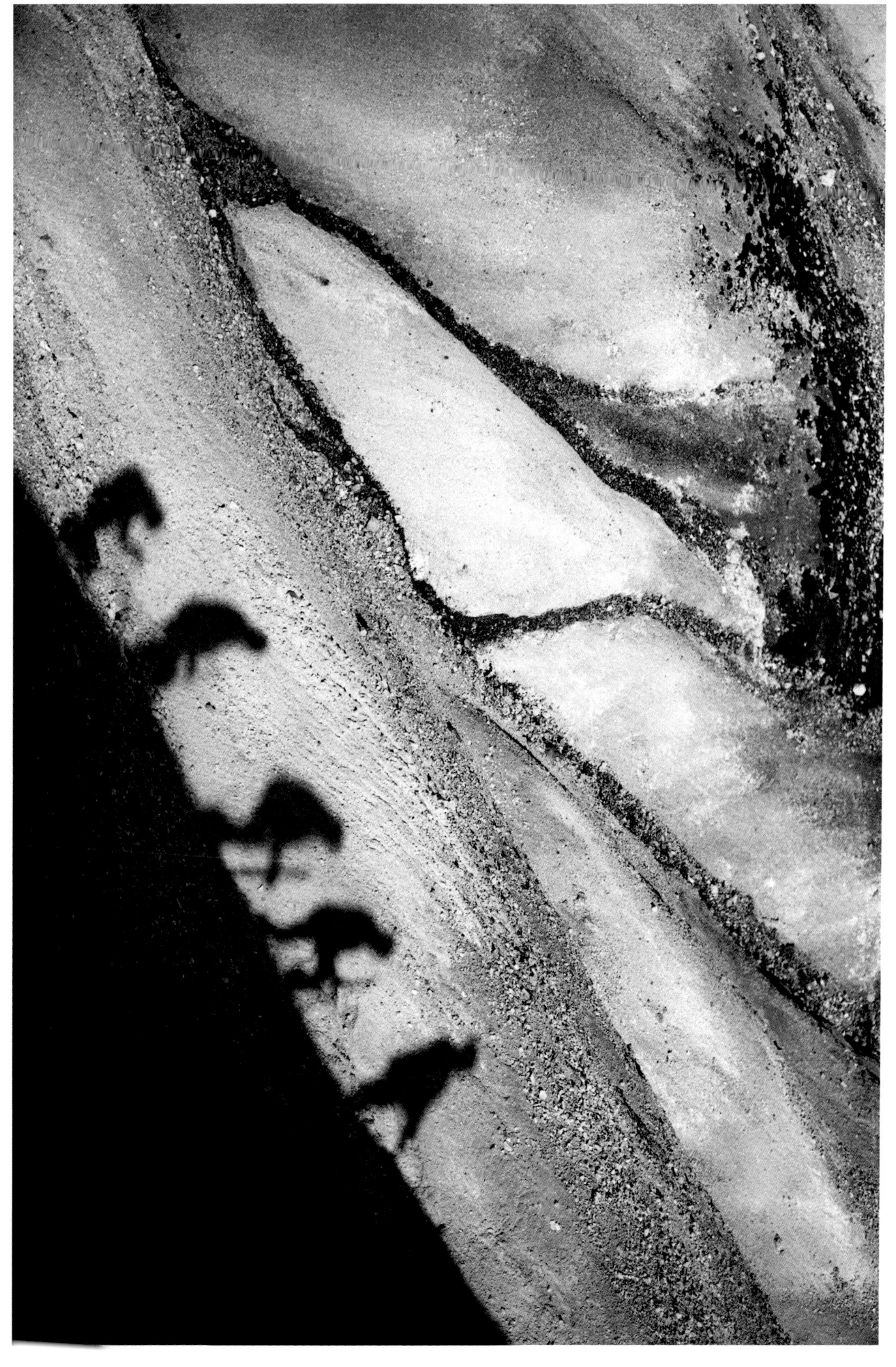

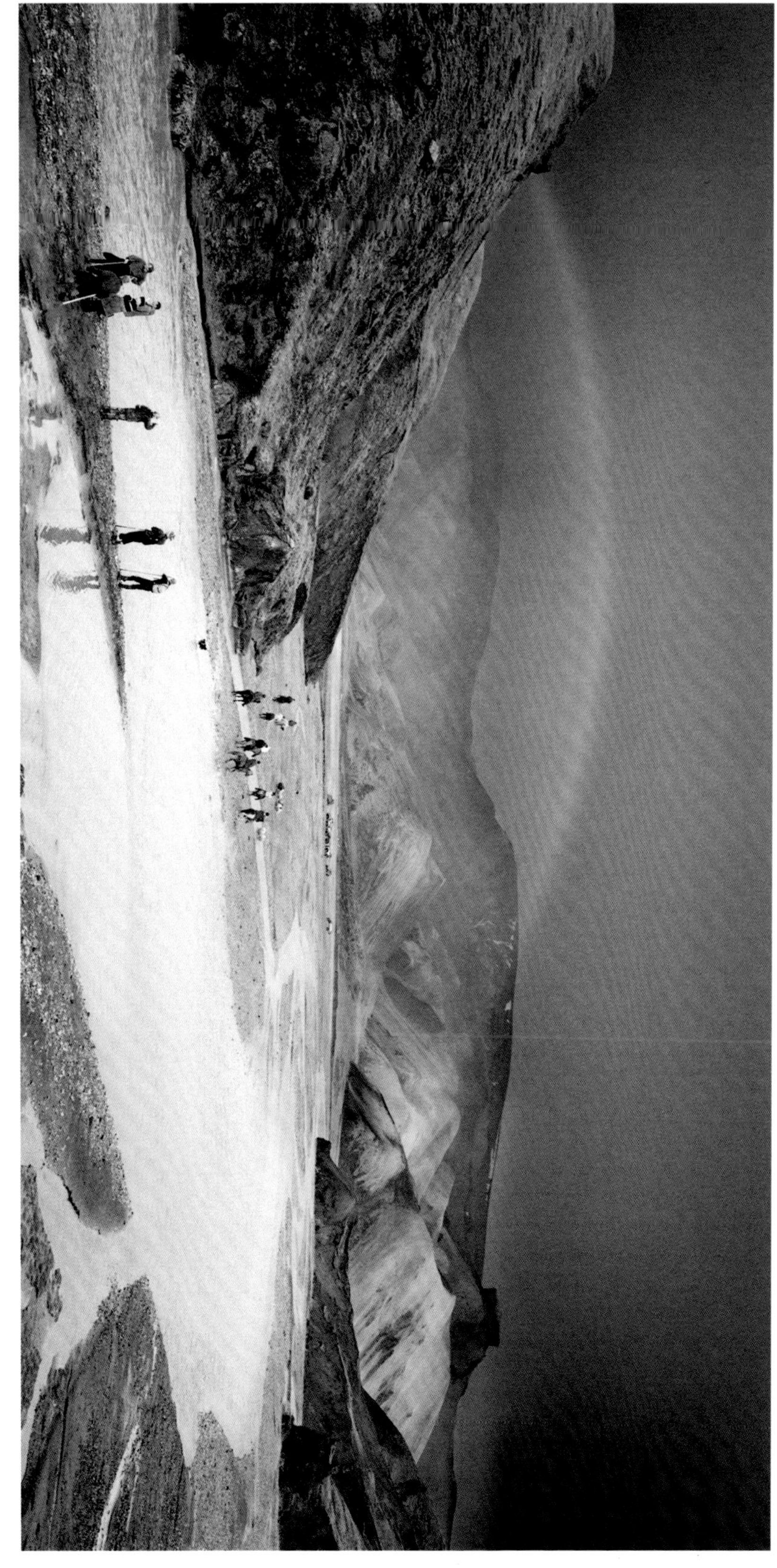

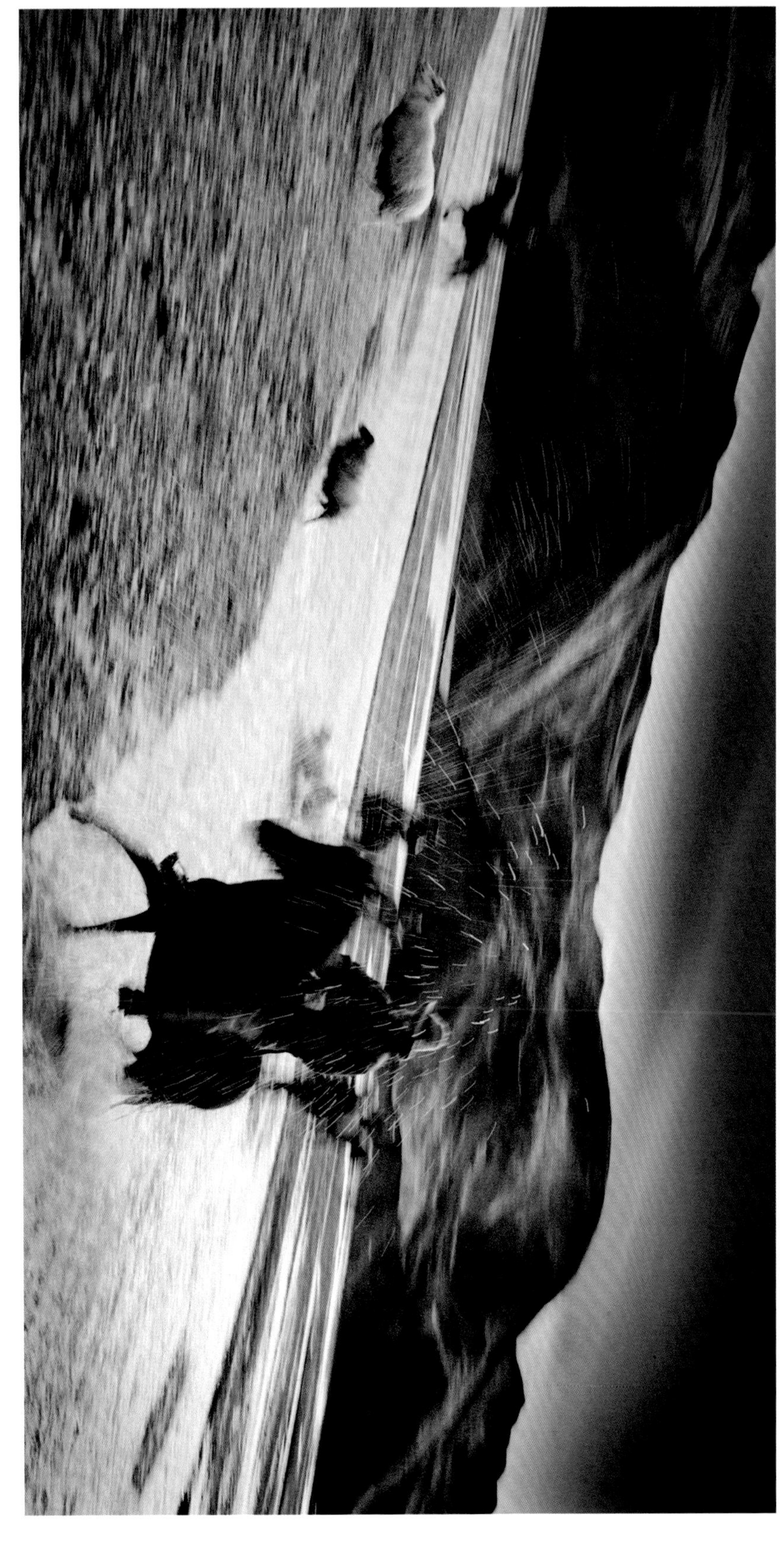

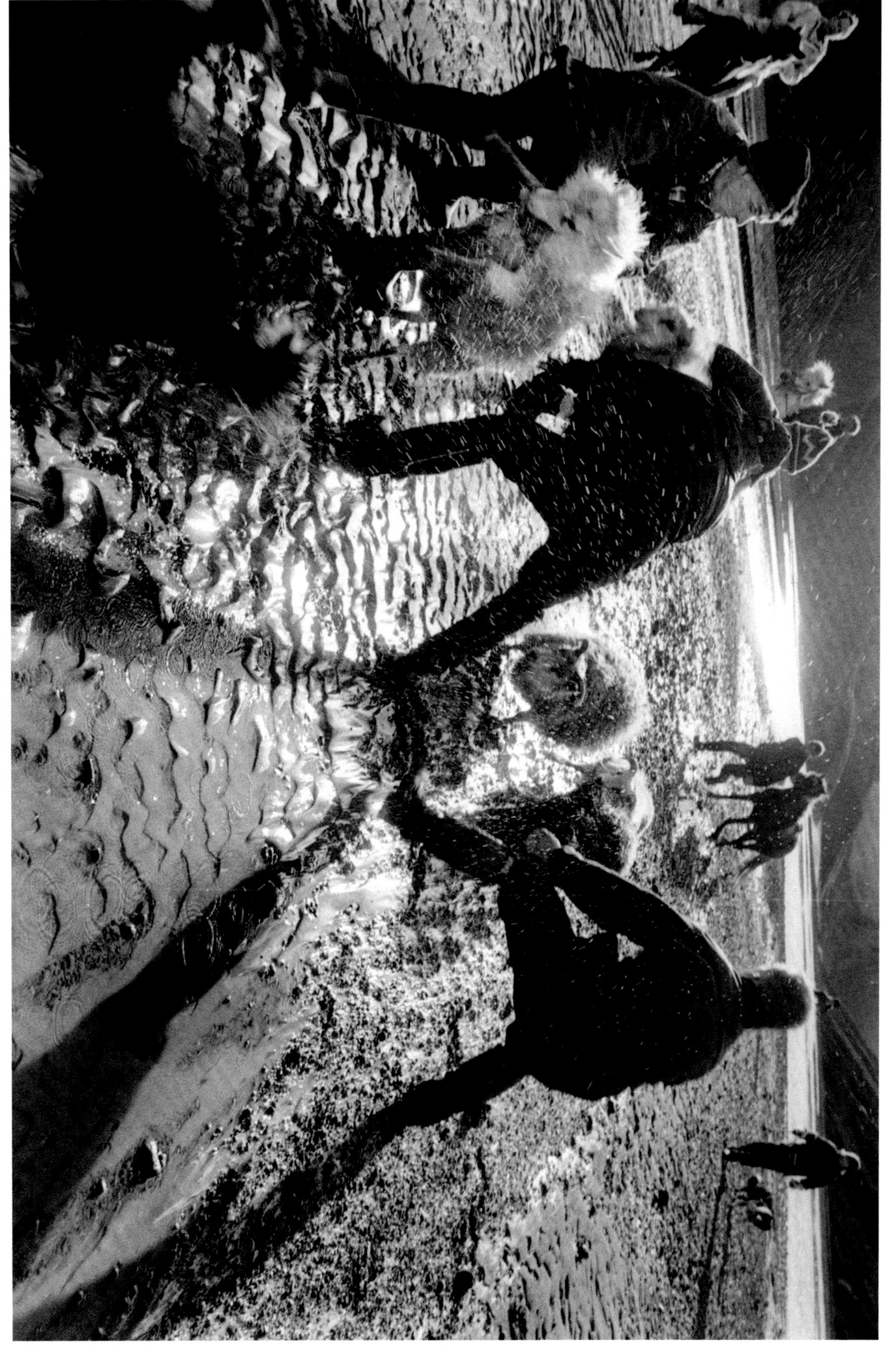

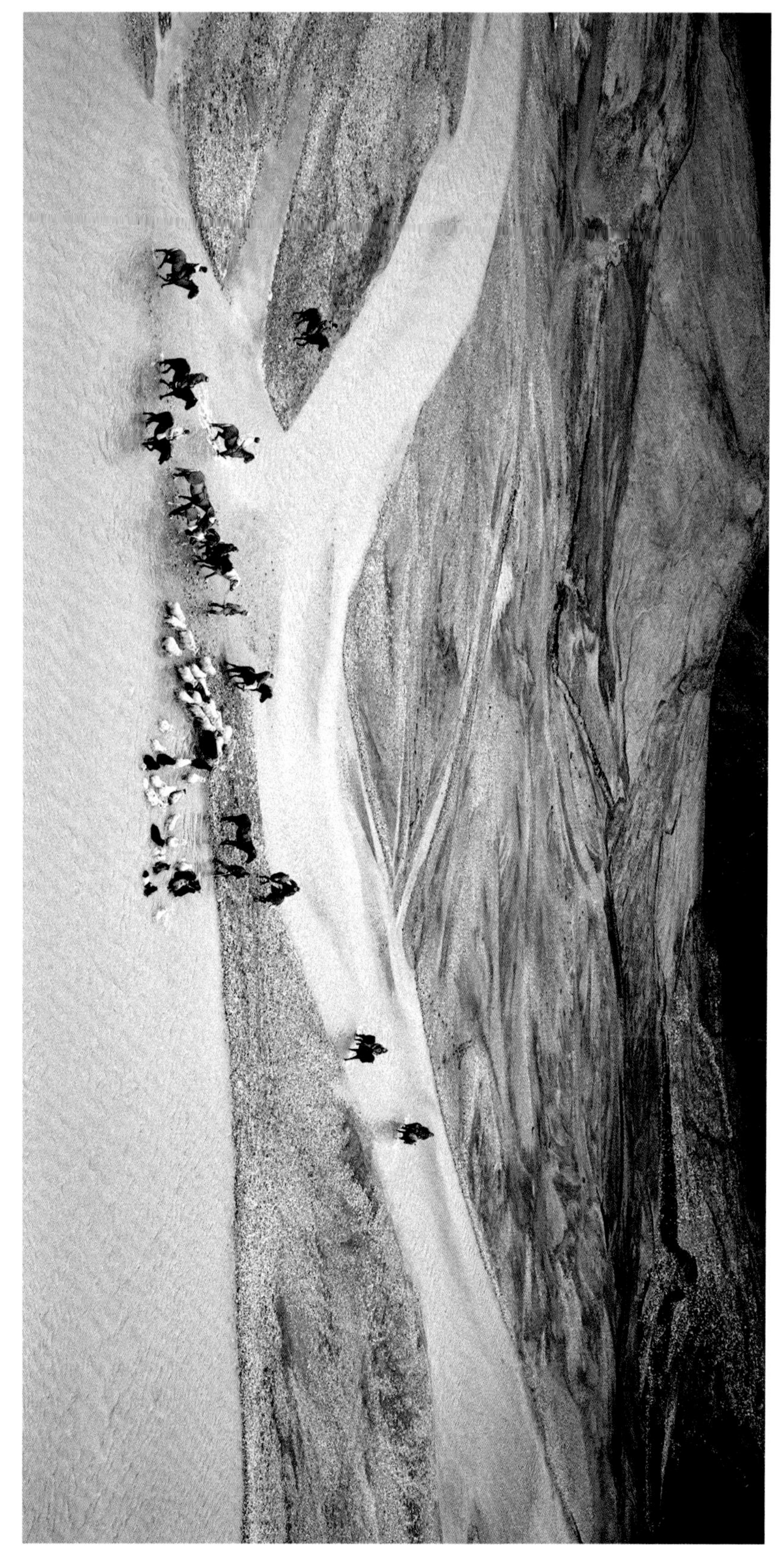

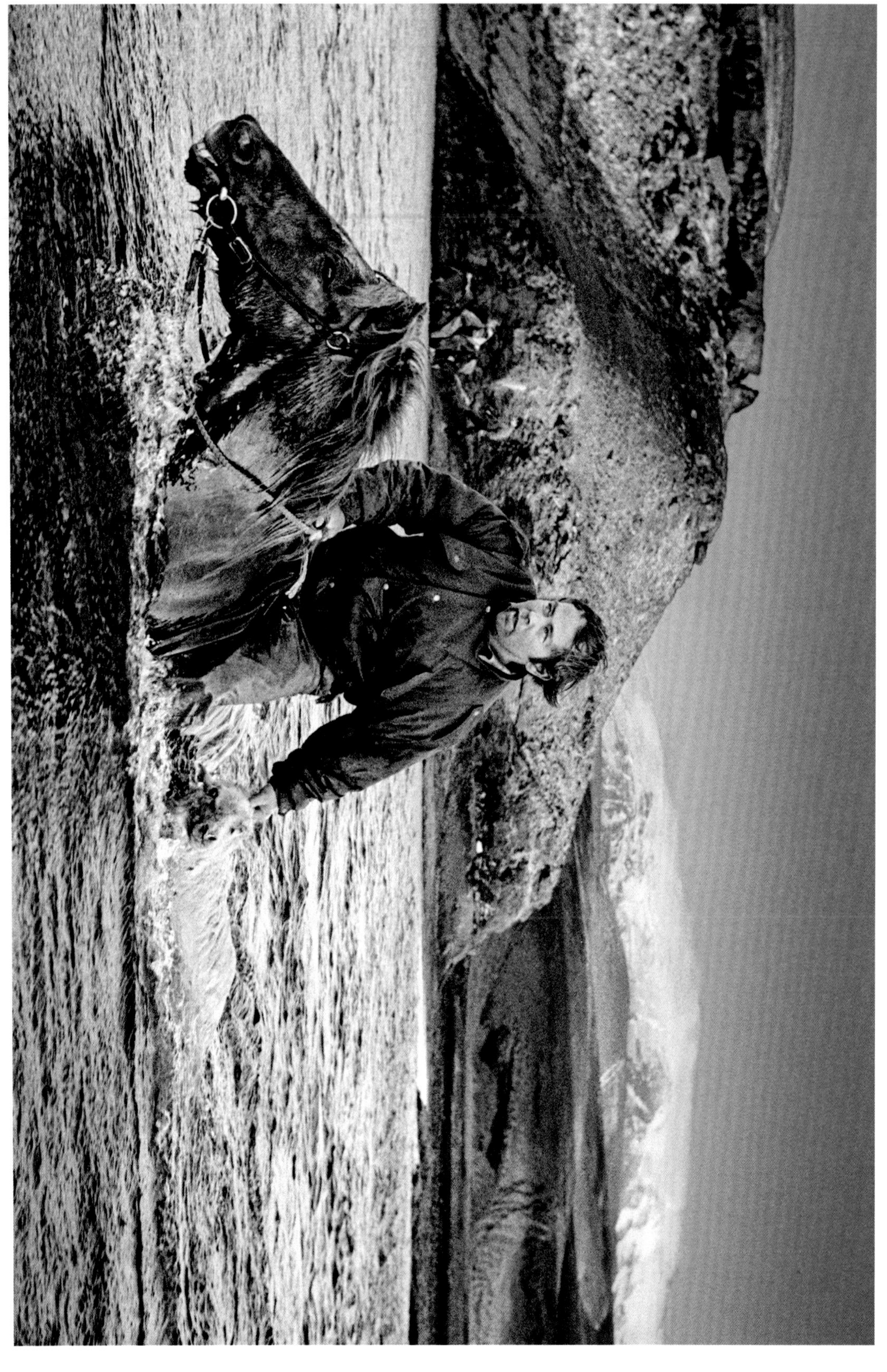

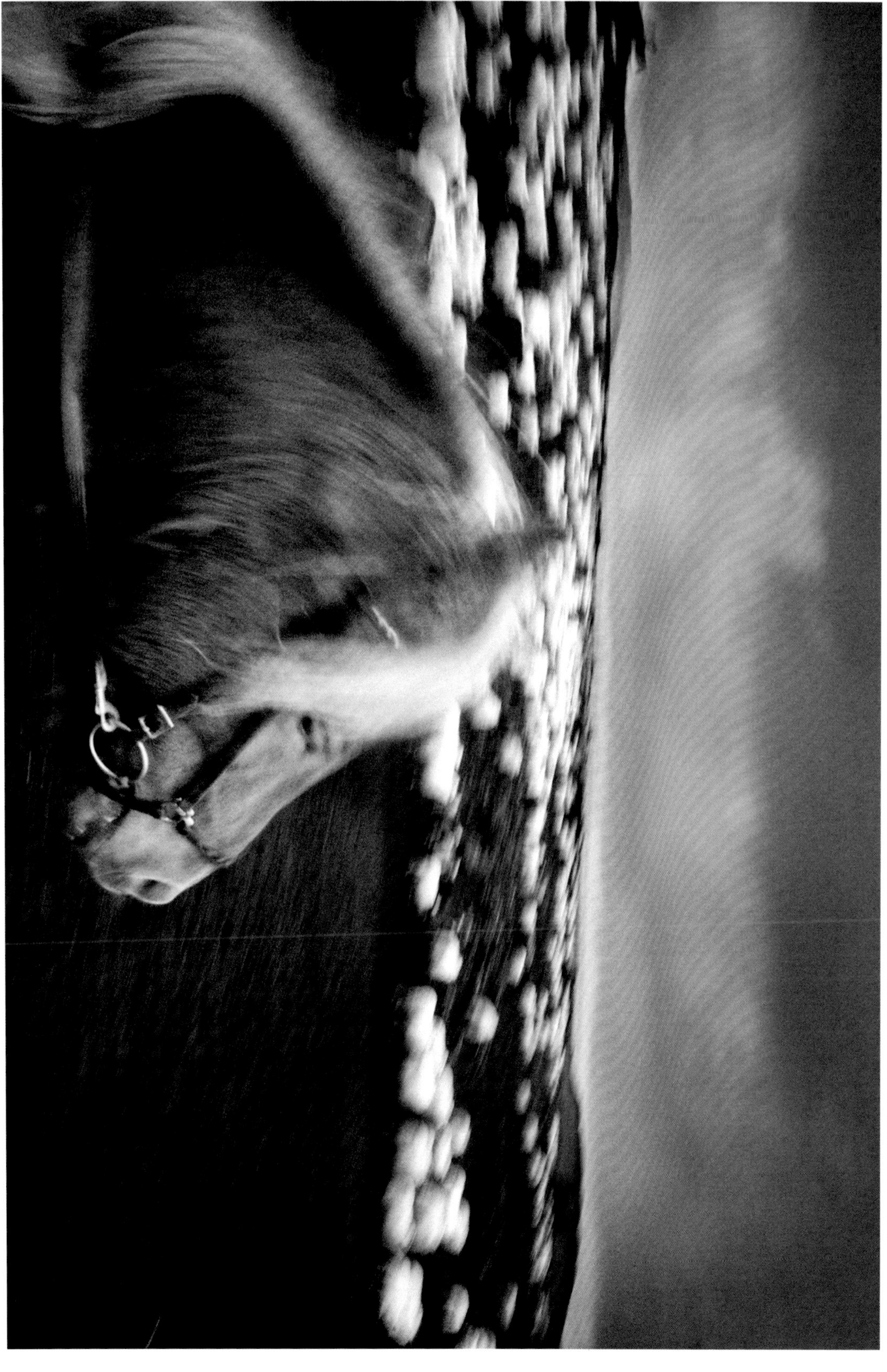

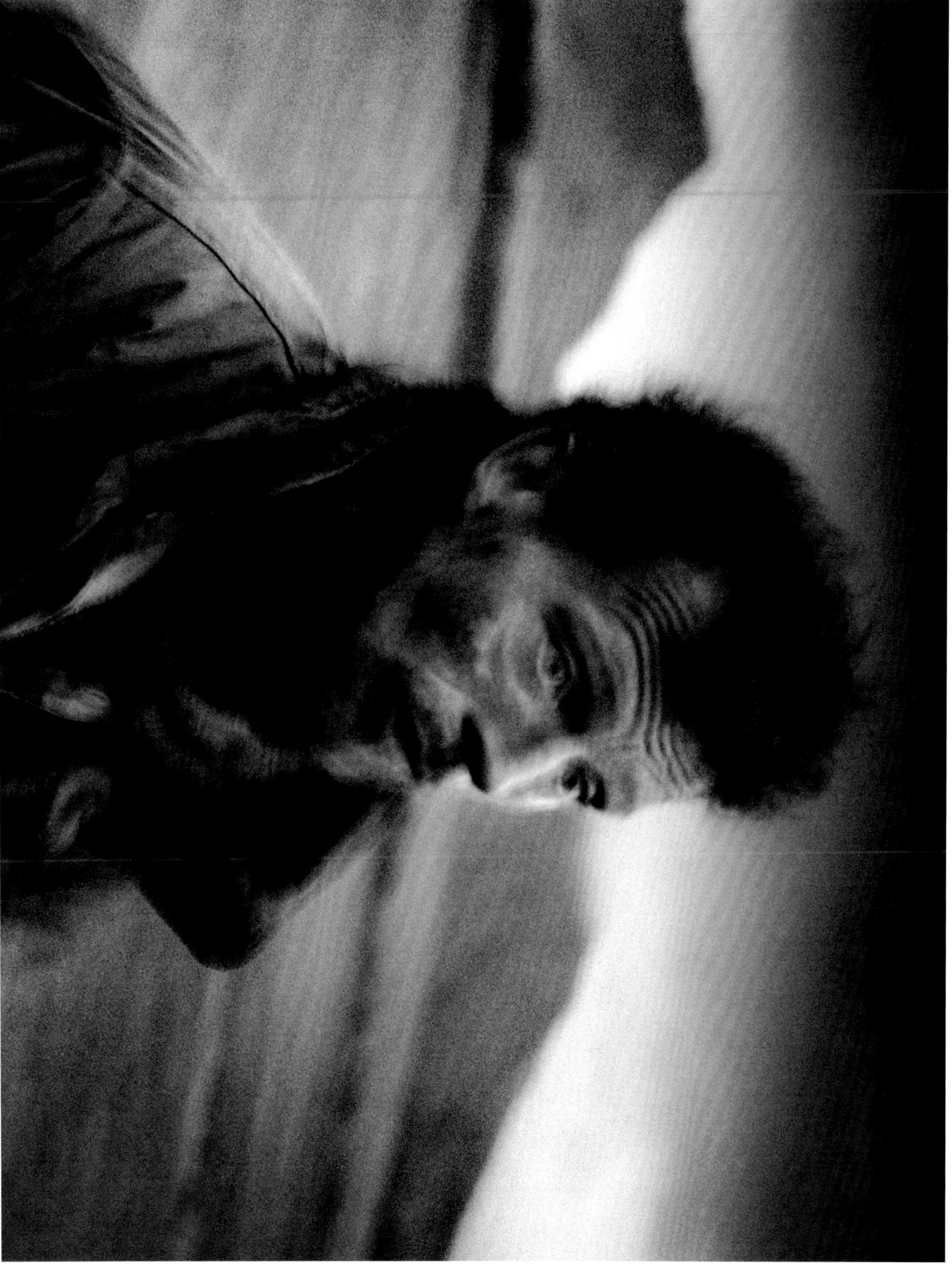

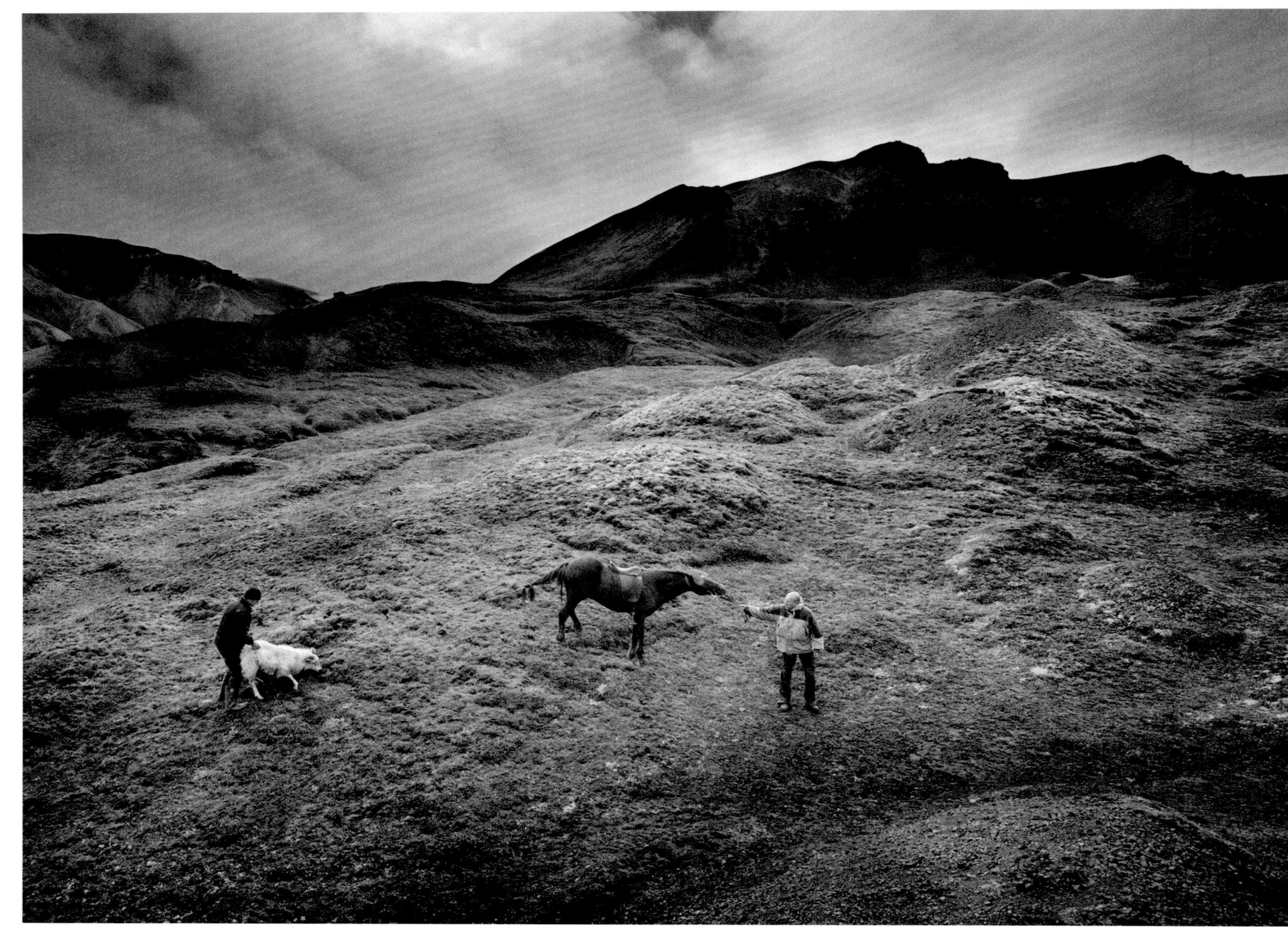

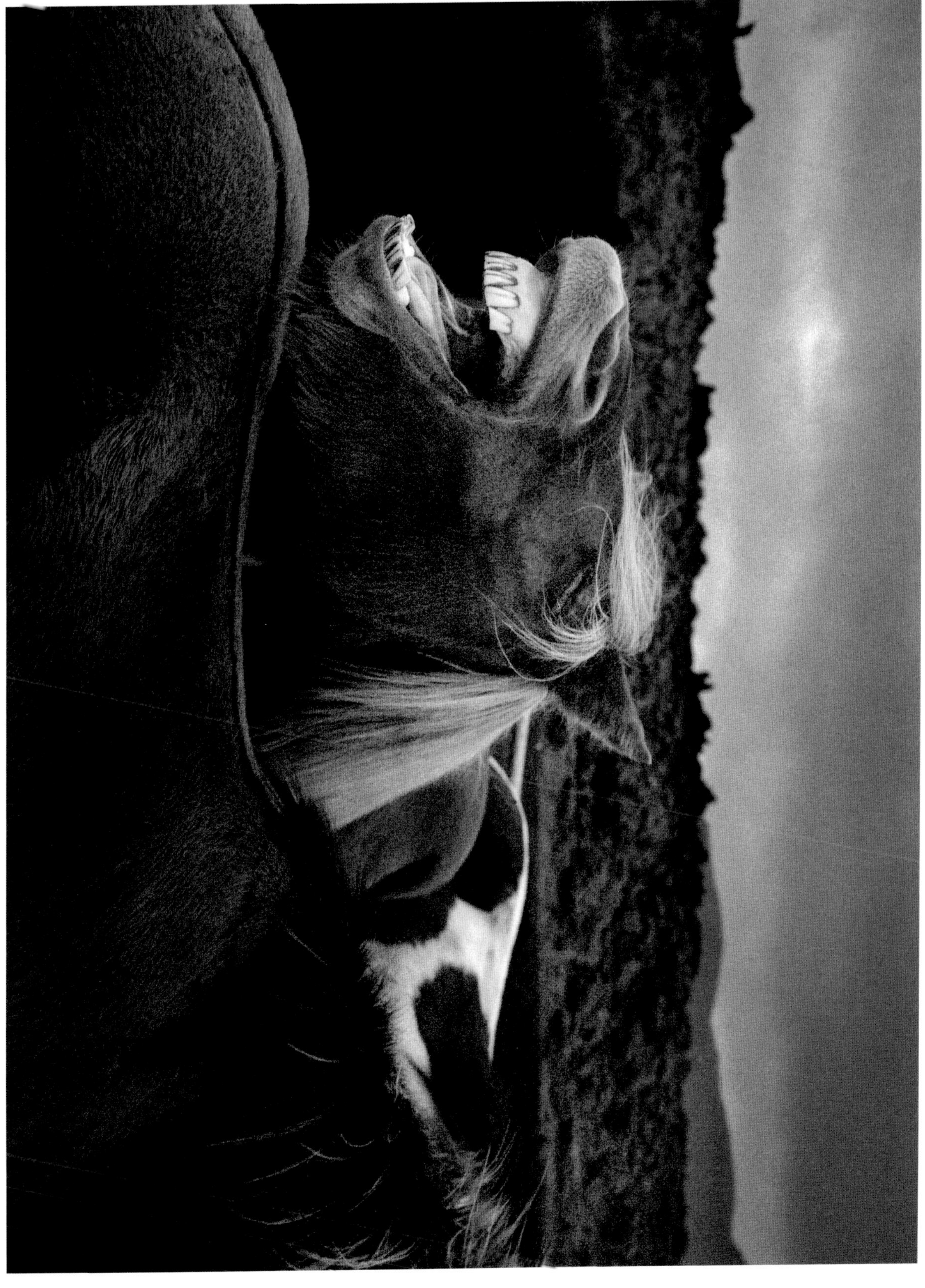

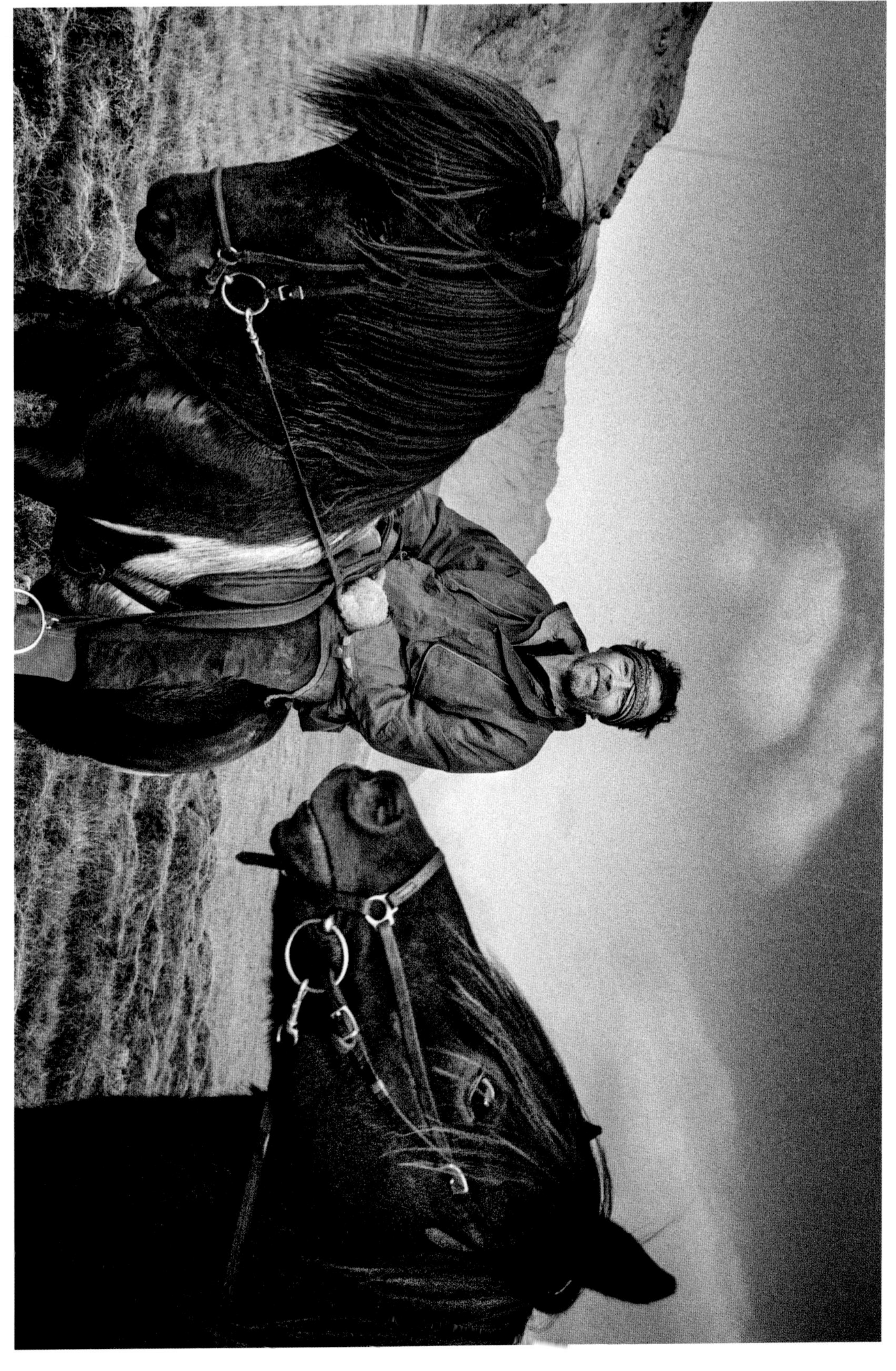

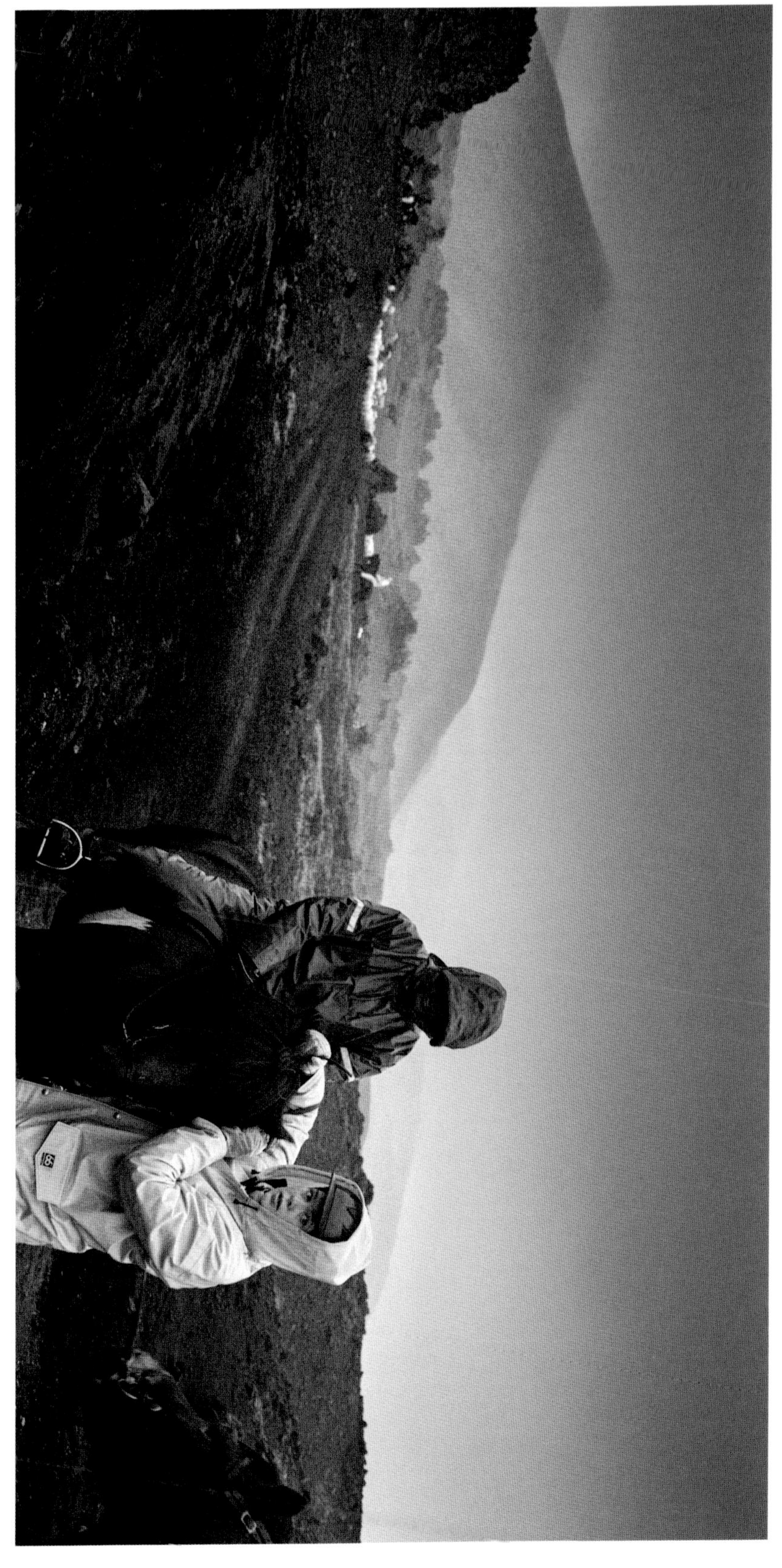

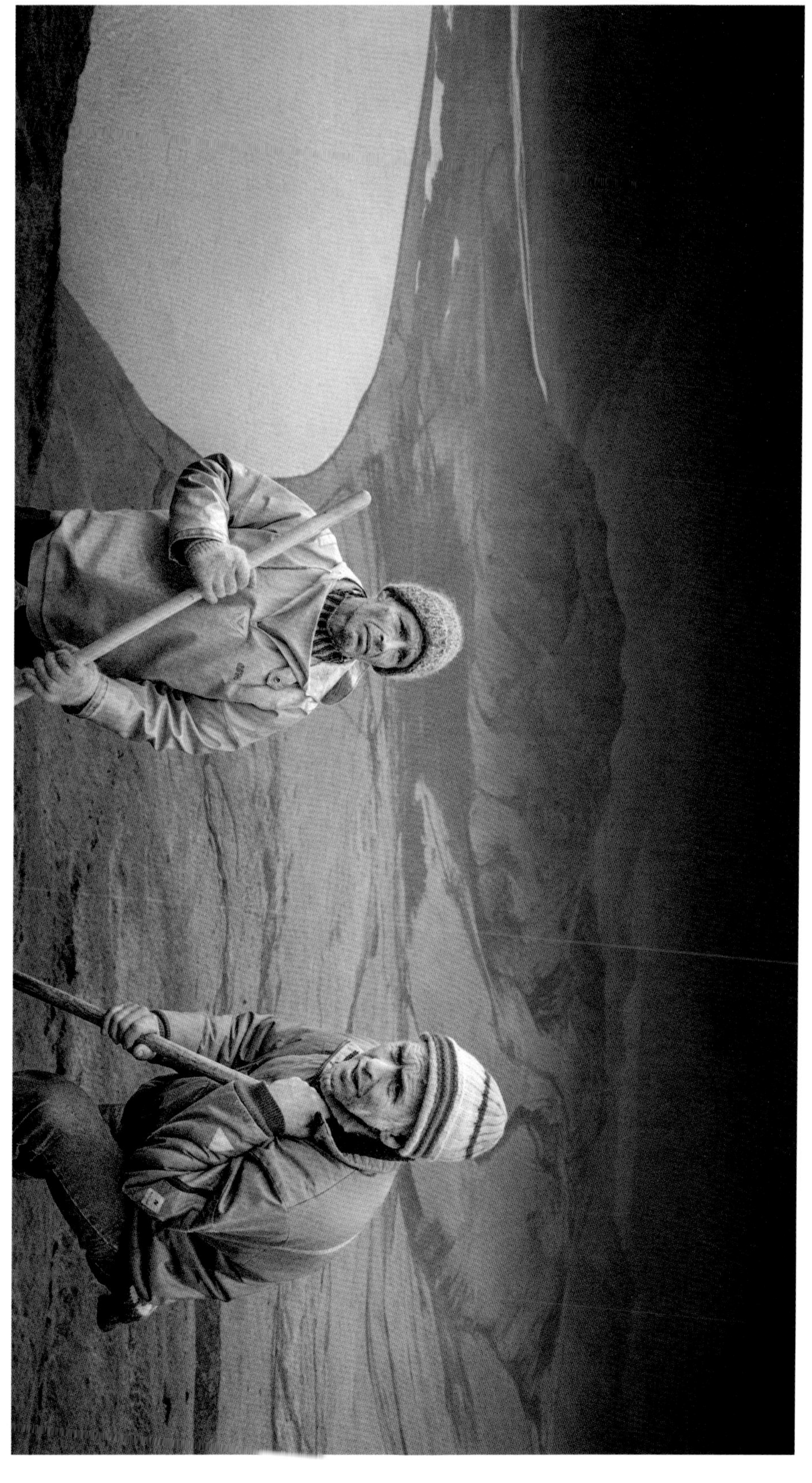

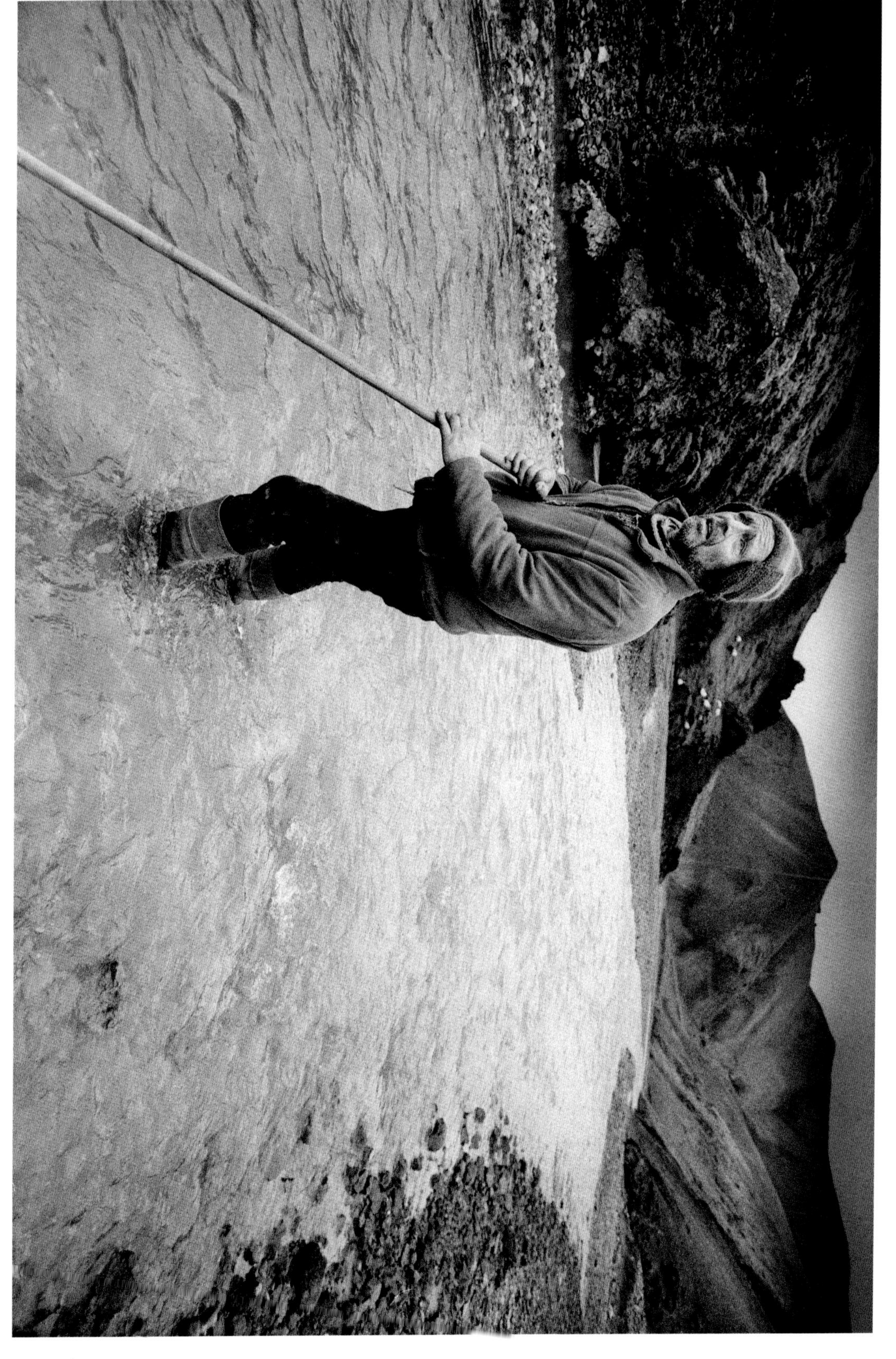

III

Weathering

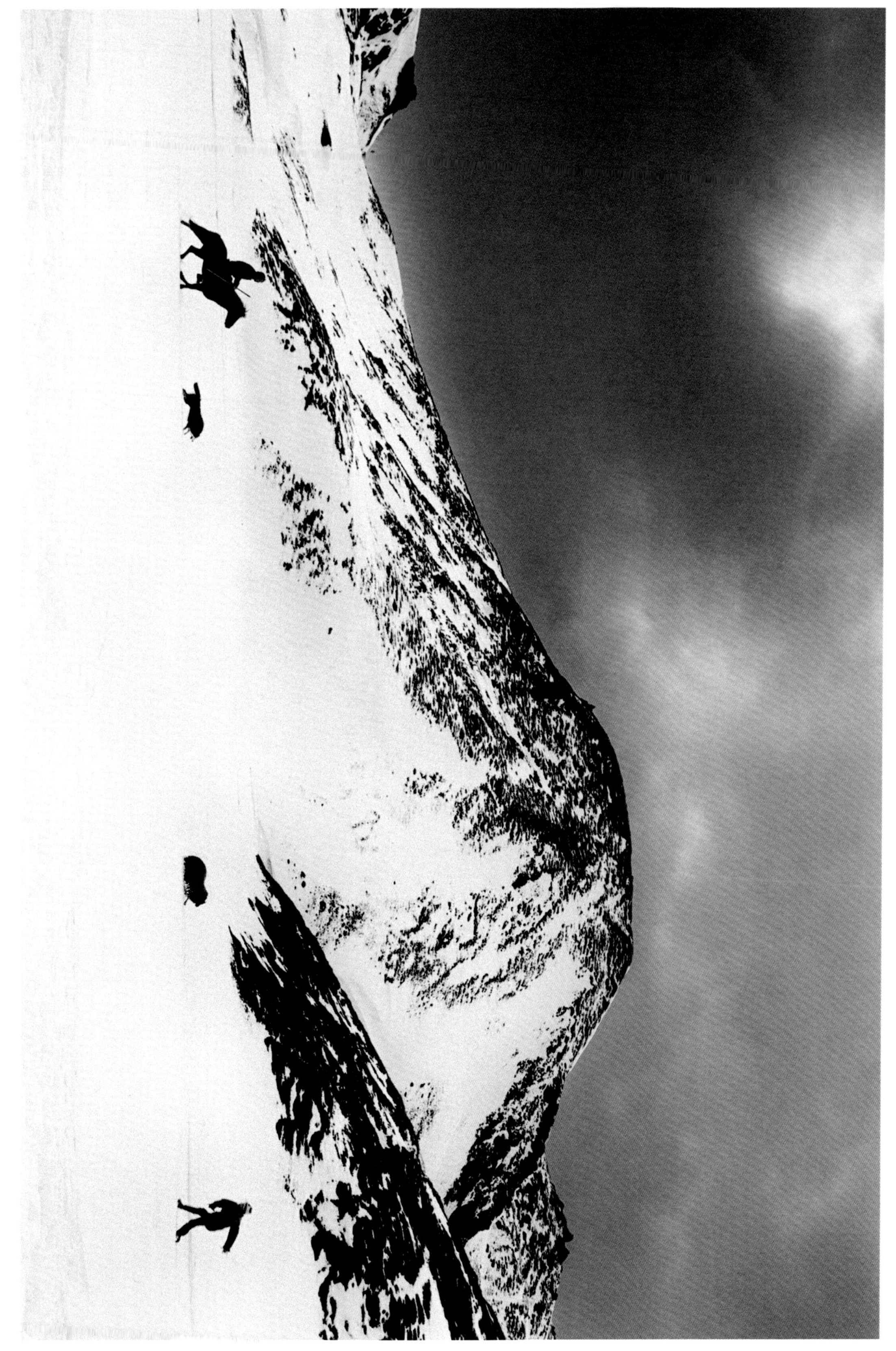

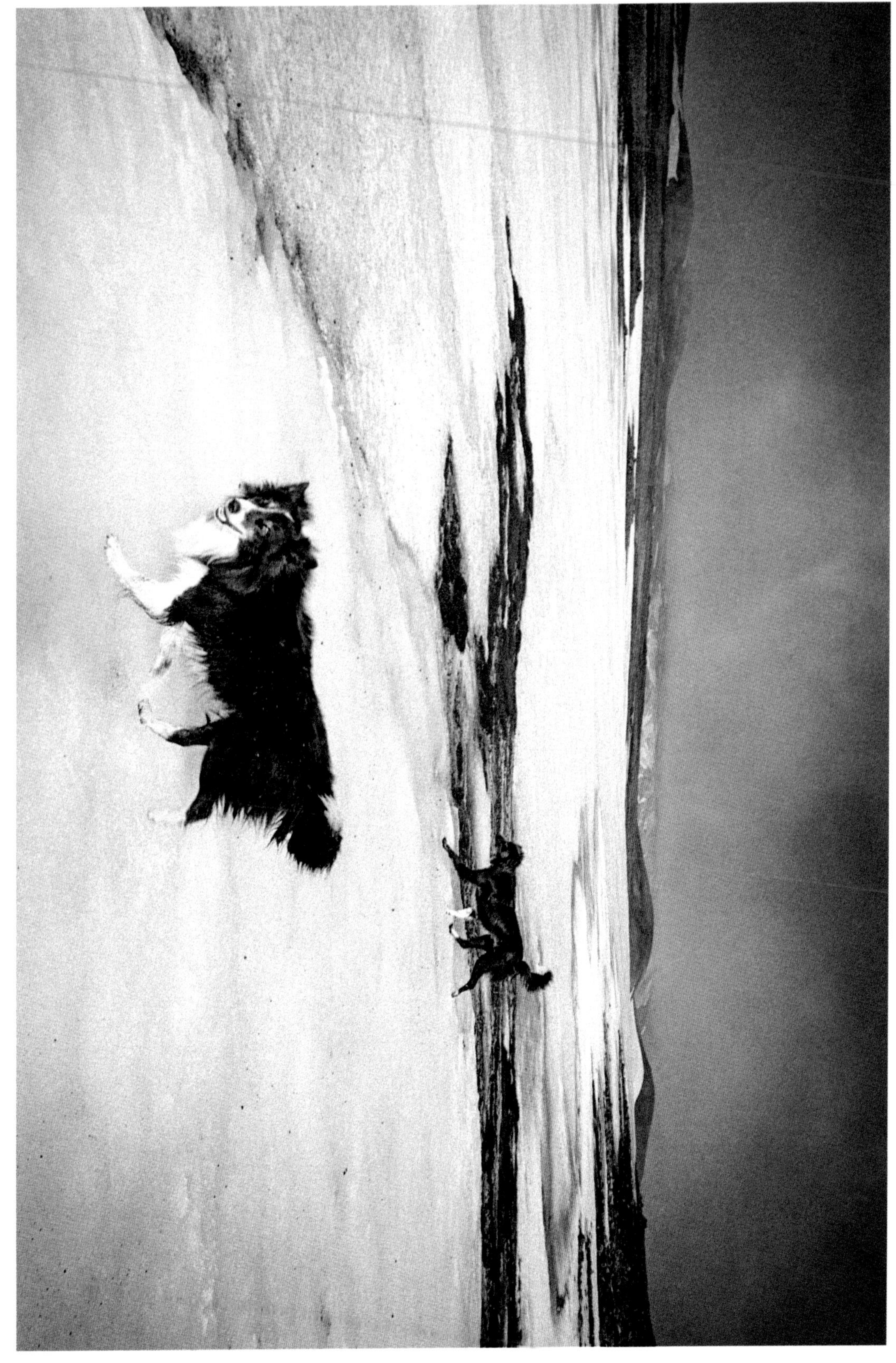

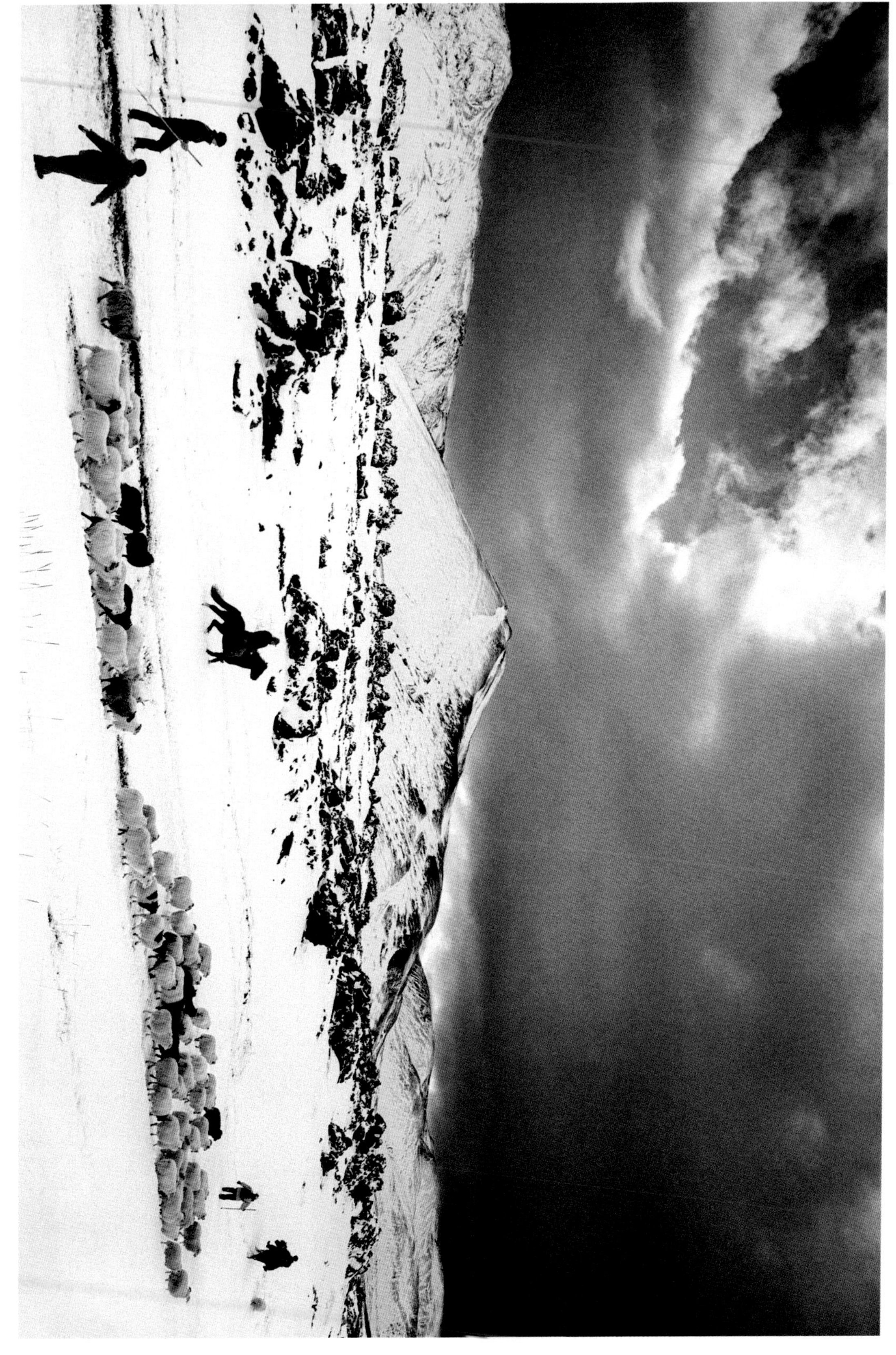

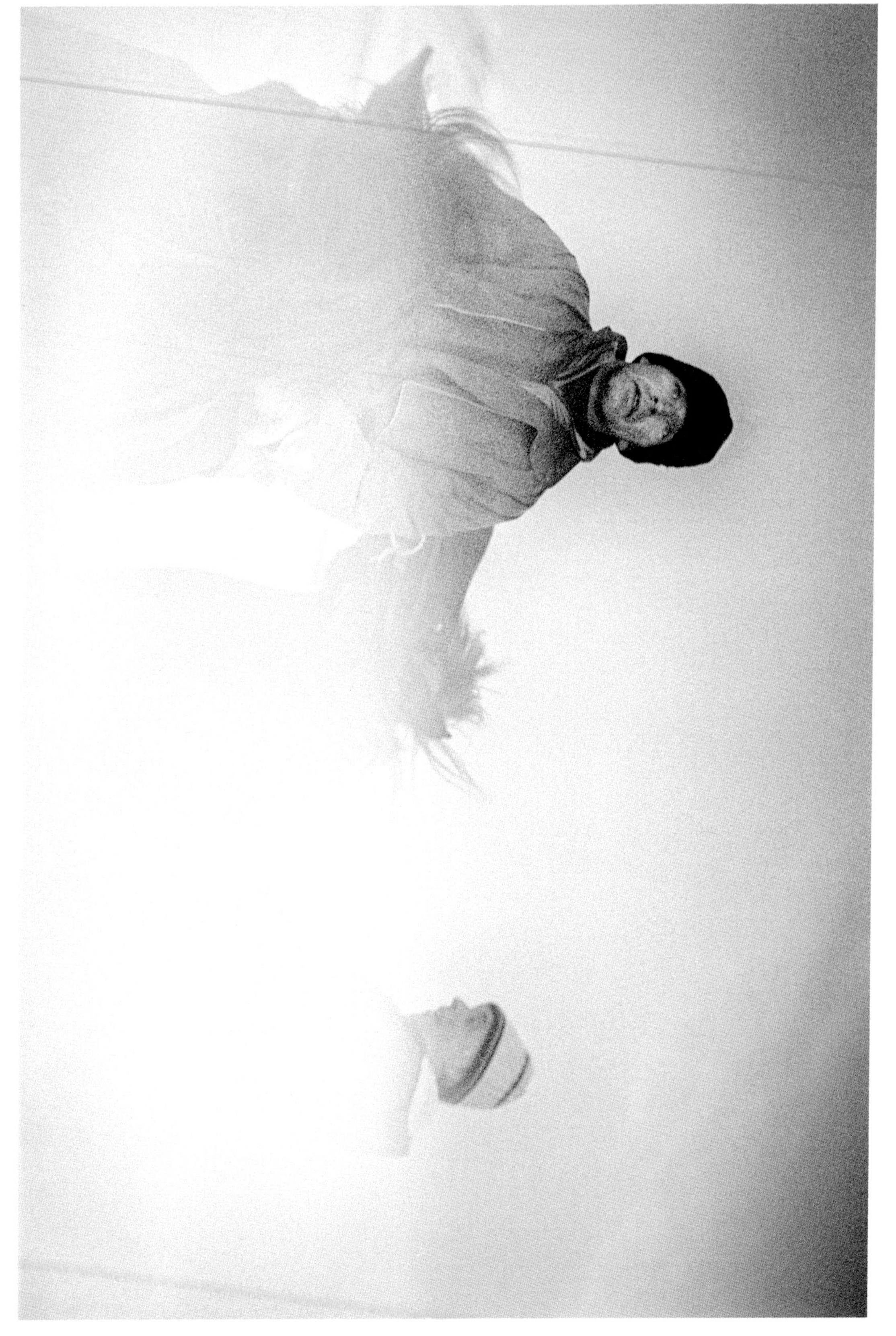

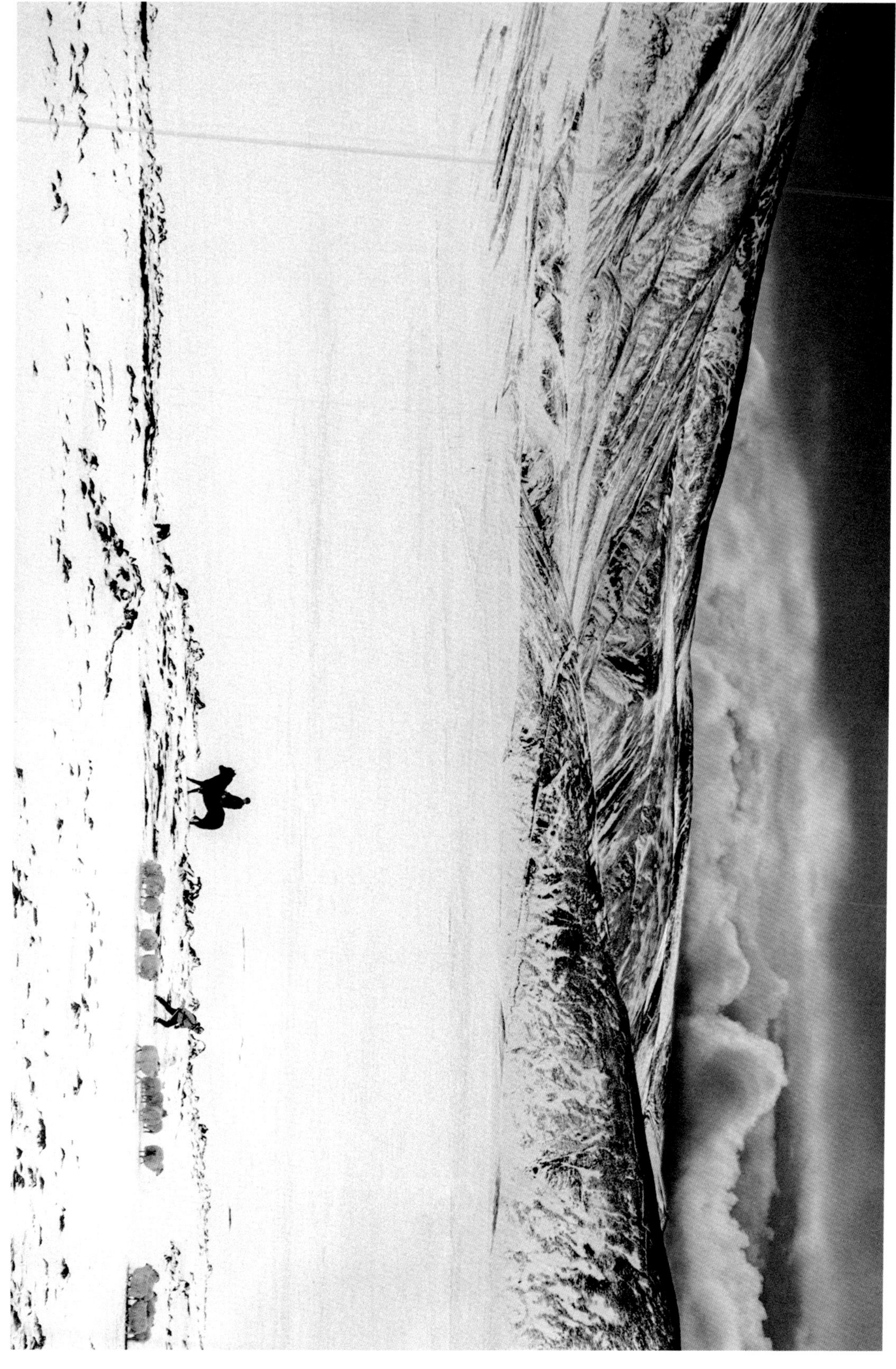

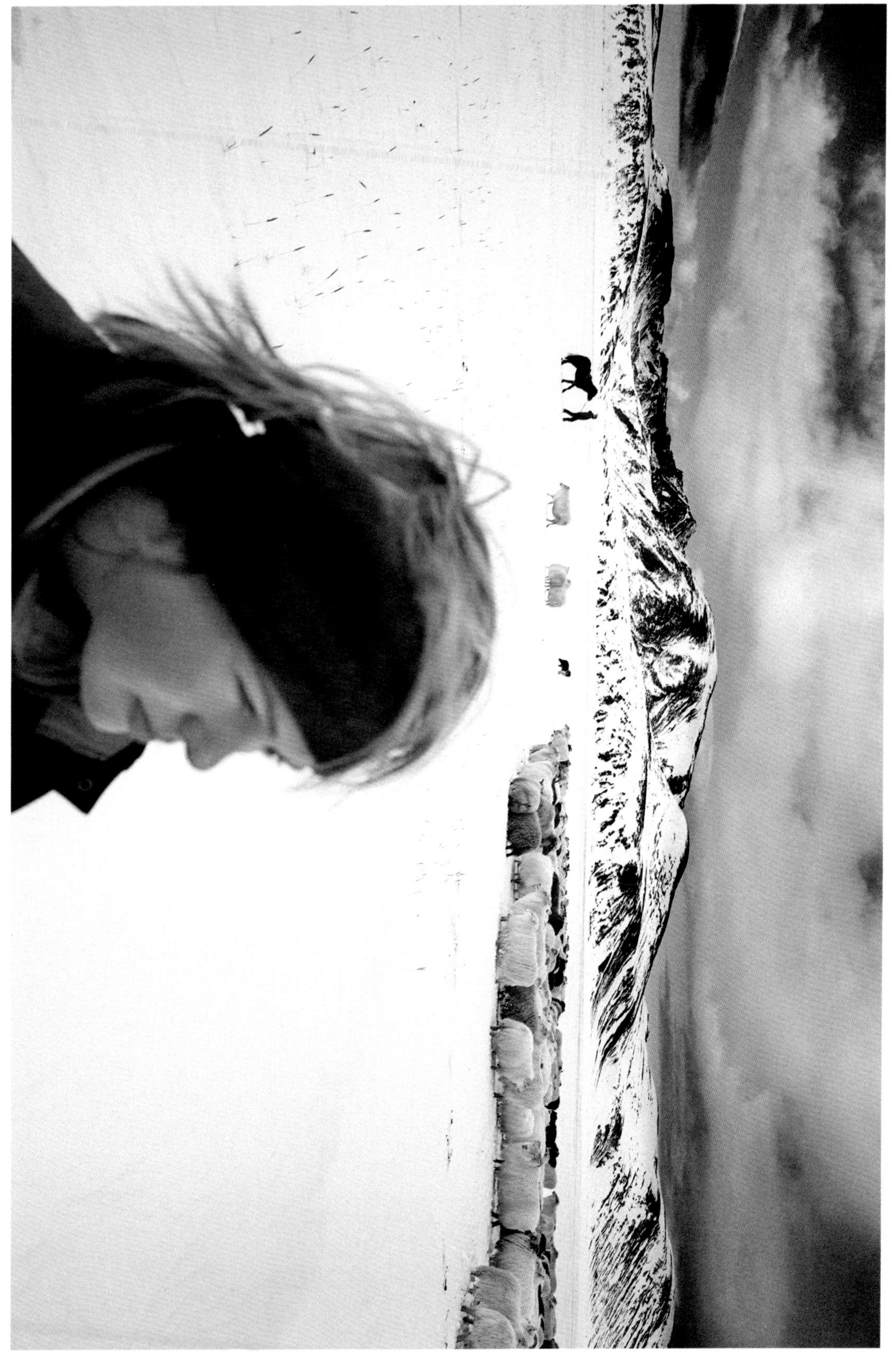

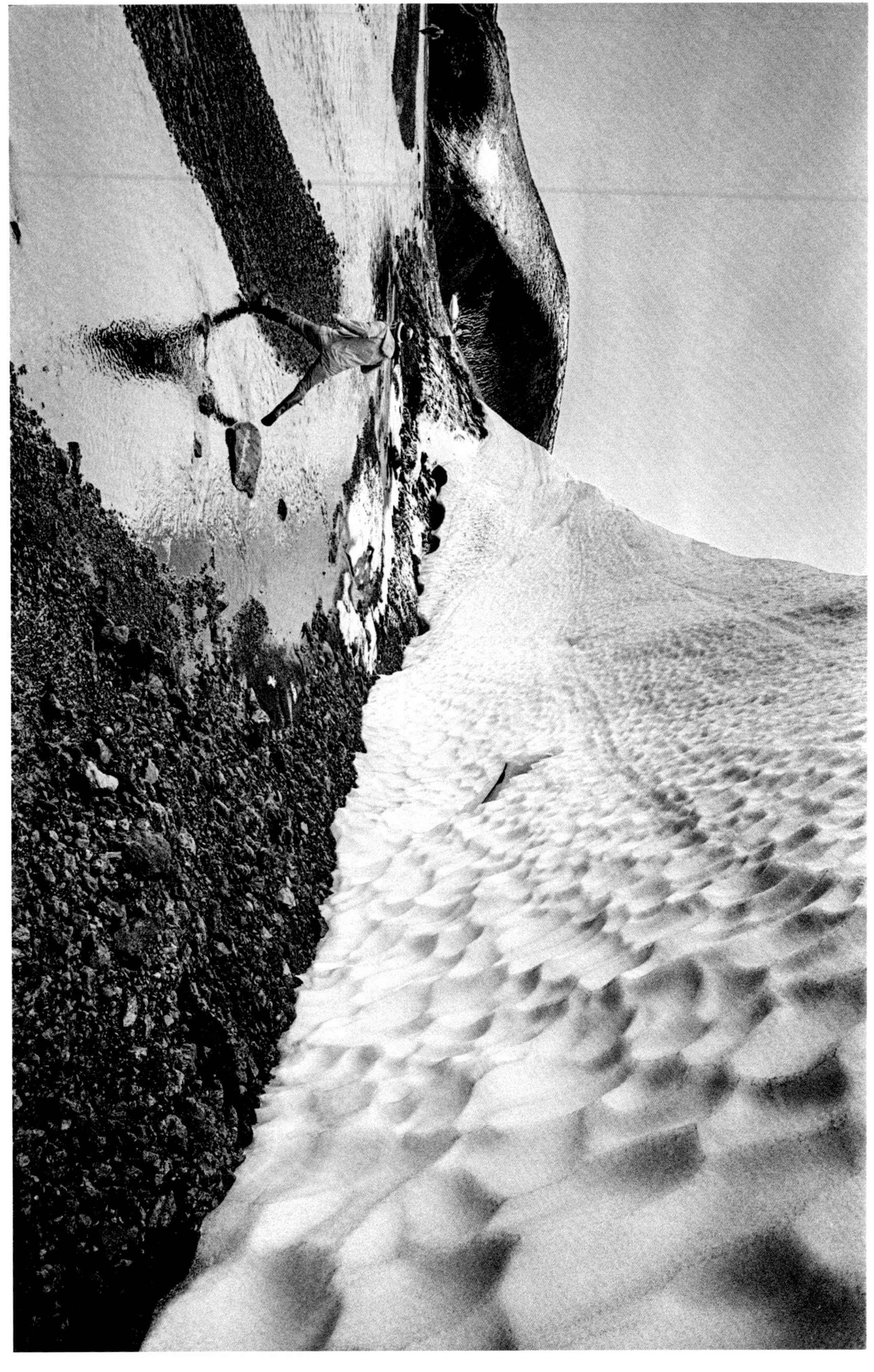

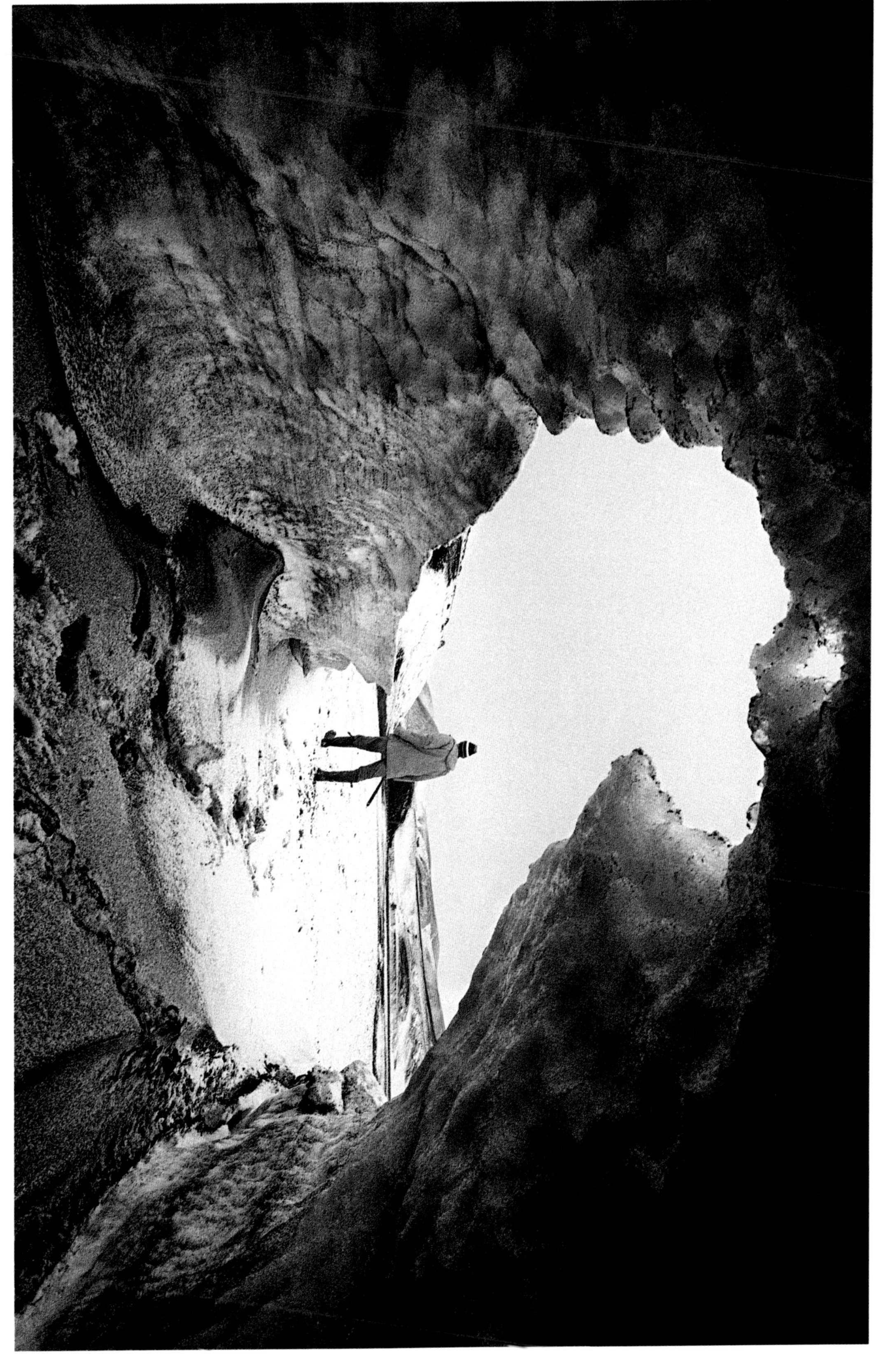

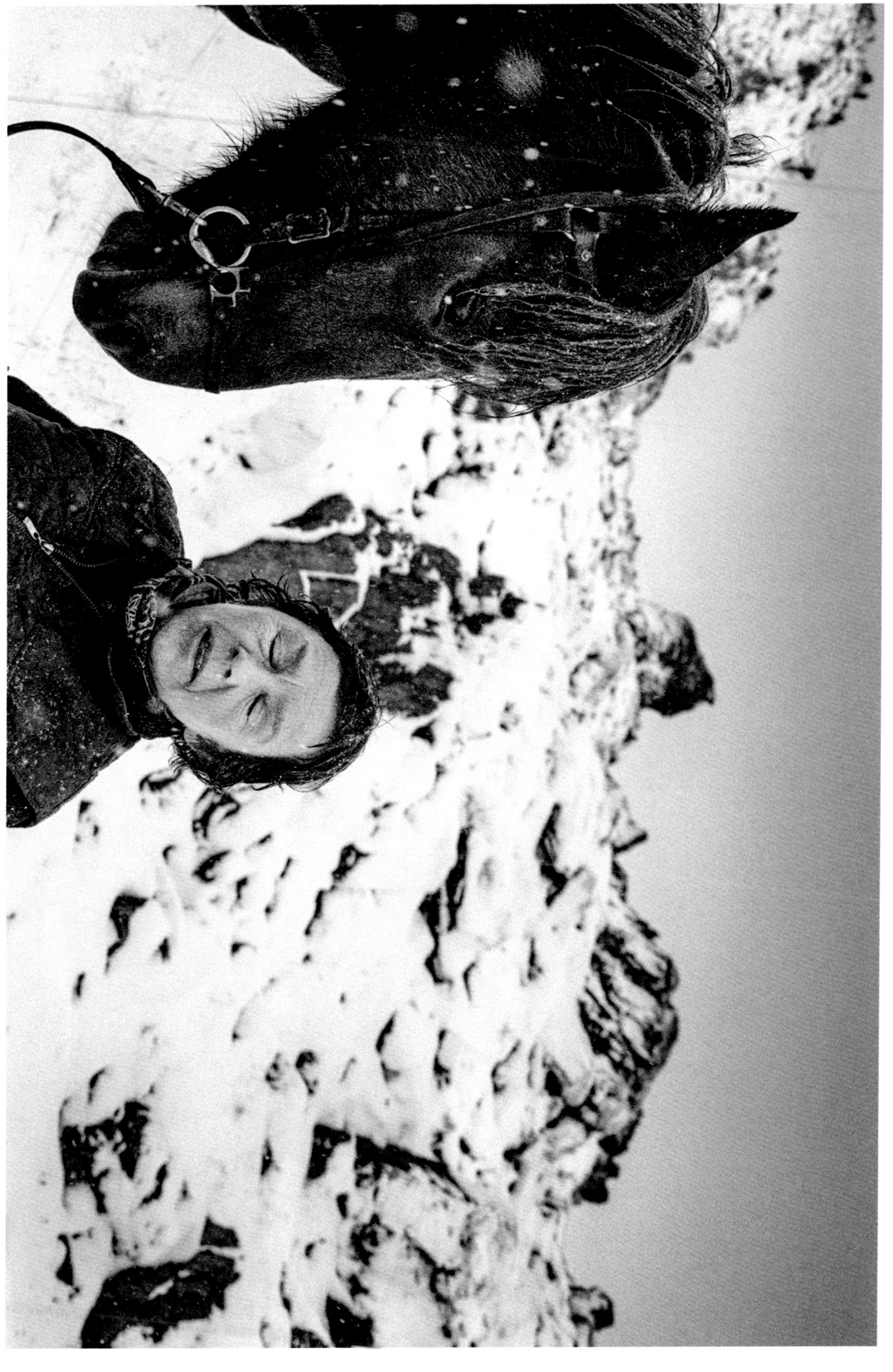

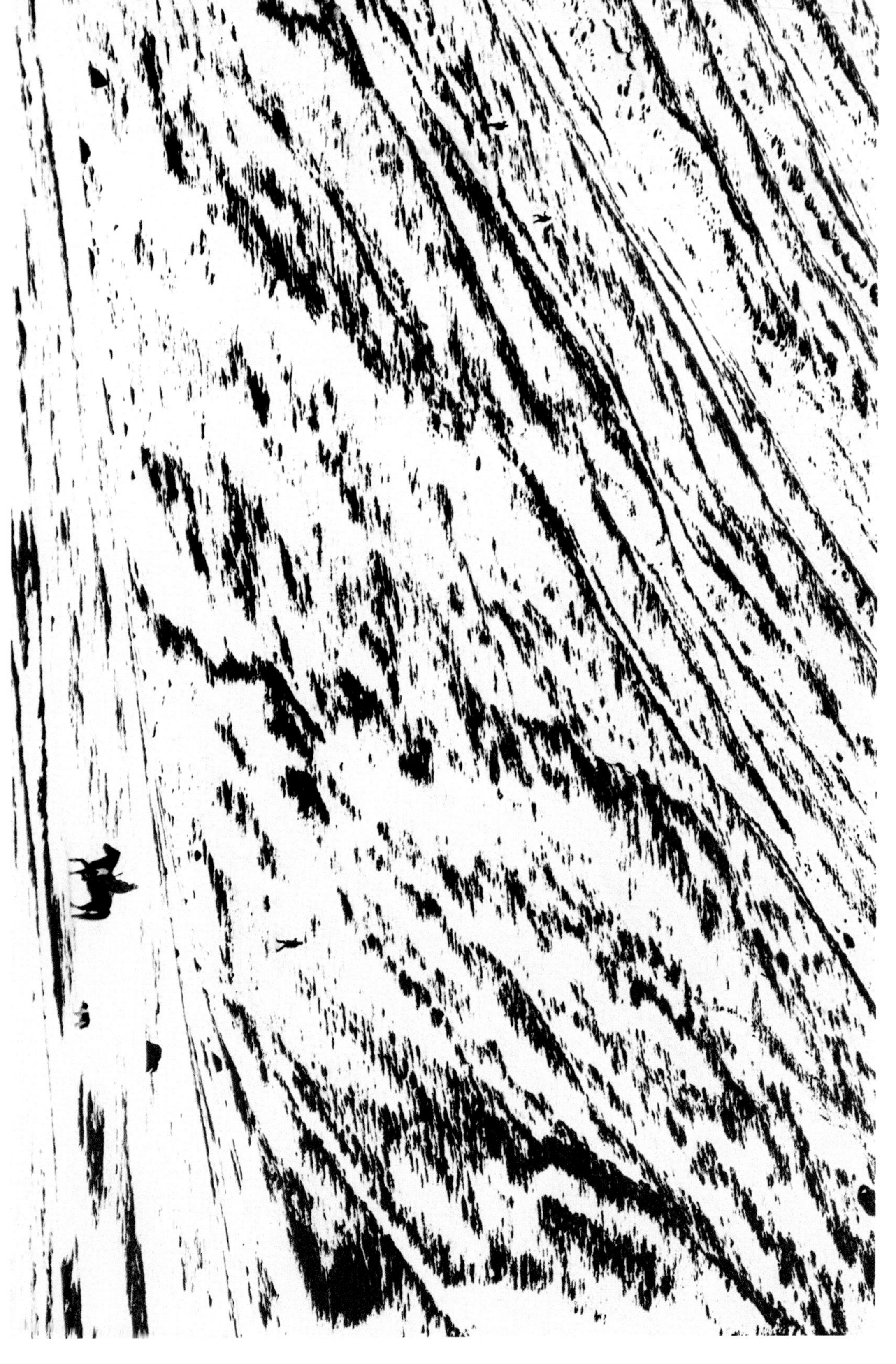

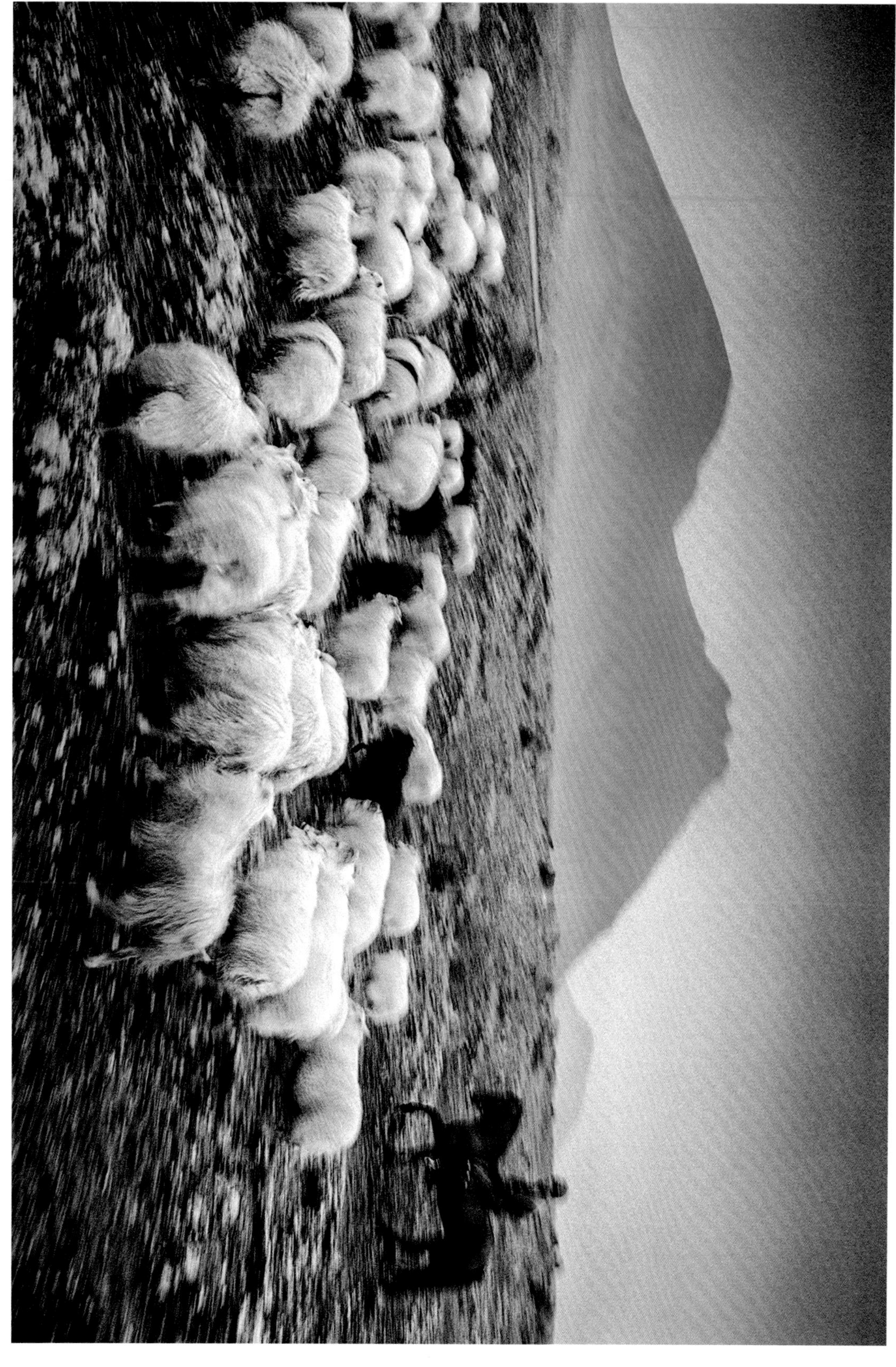

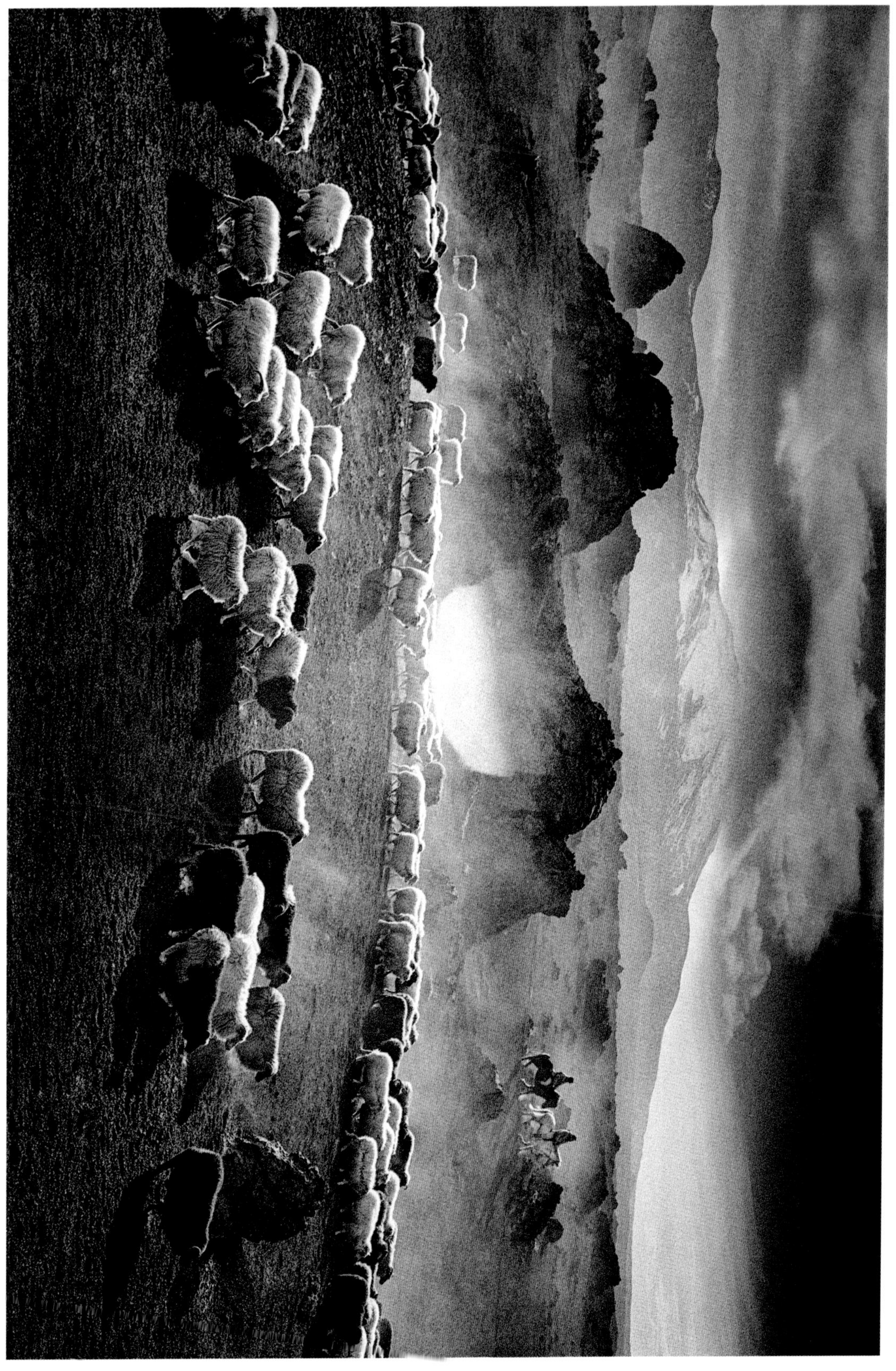

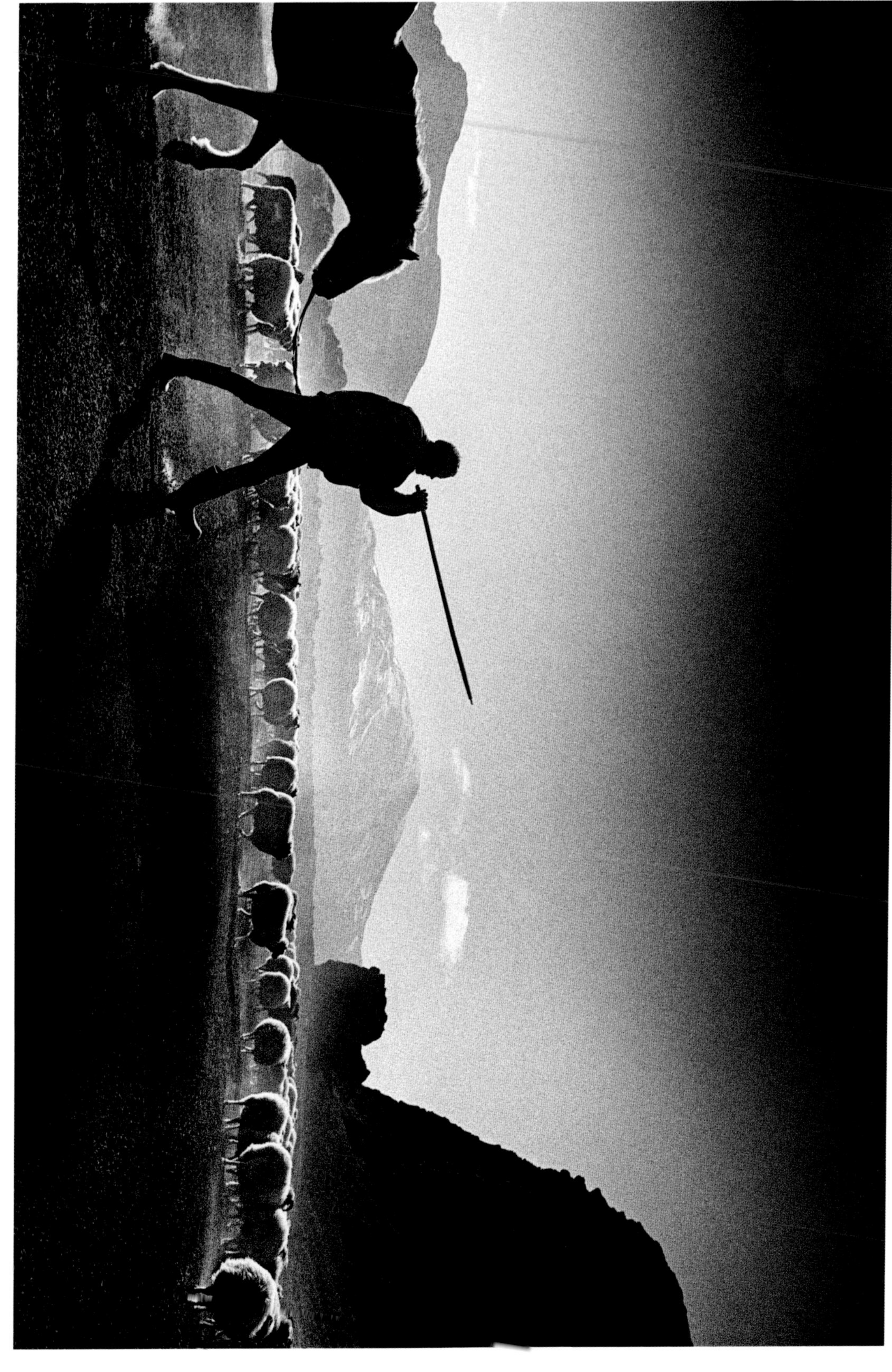

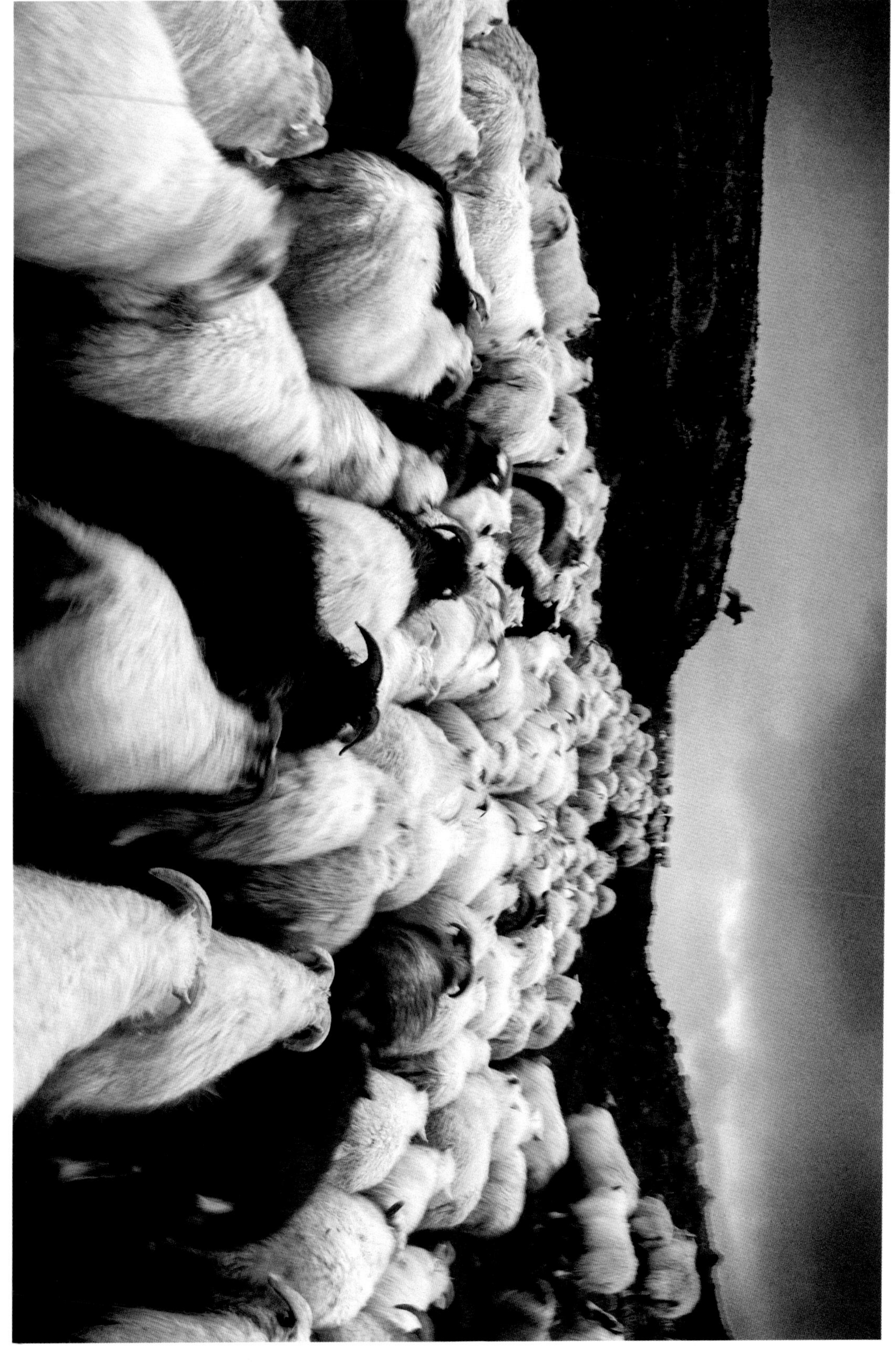

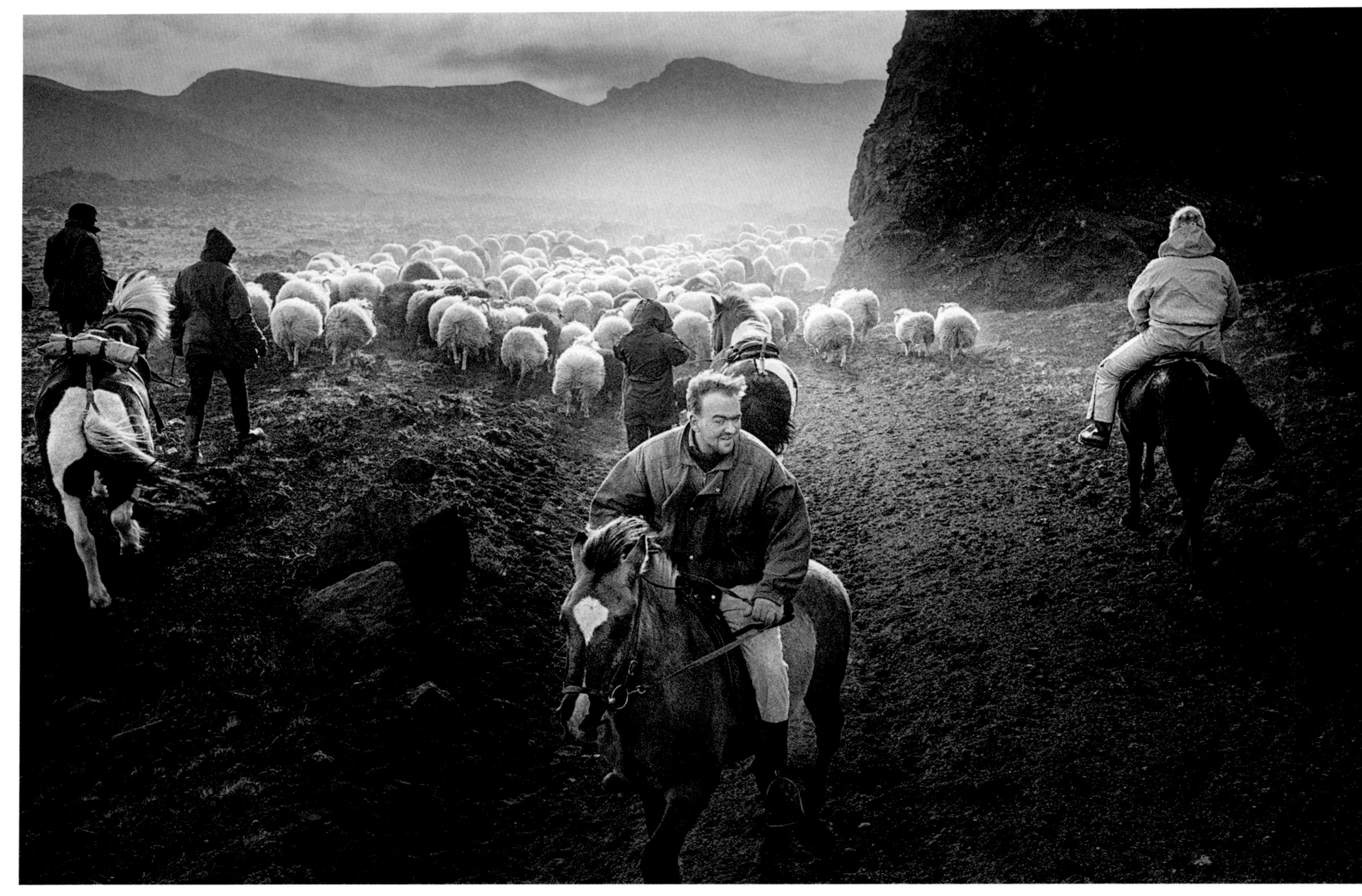

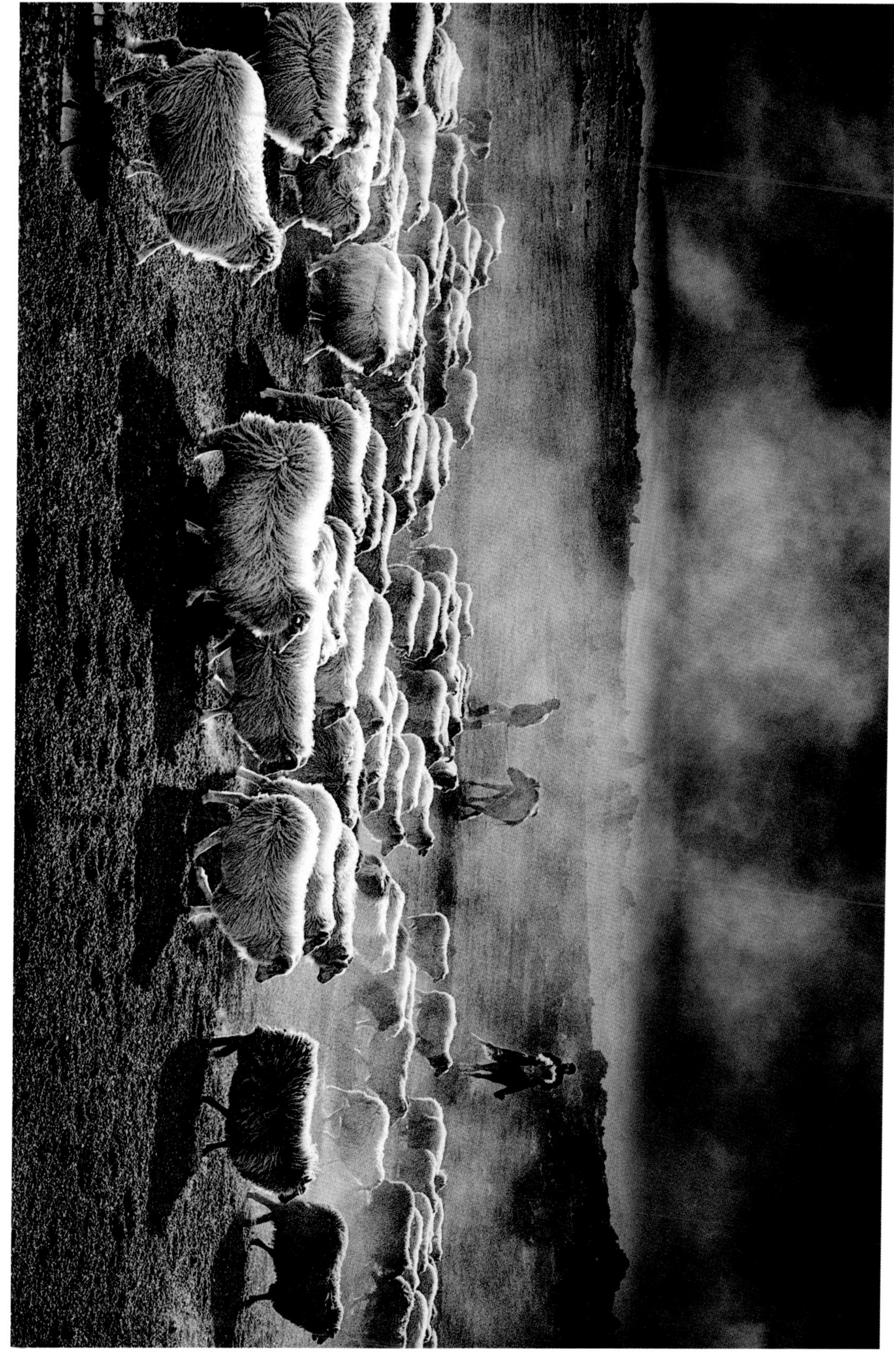

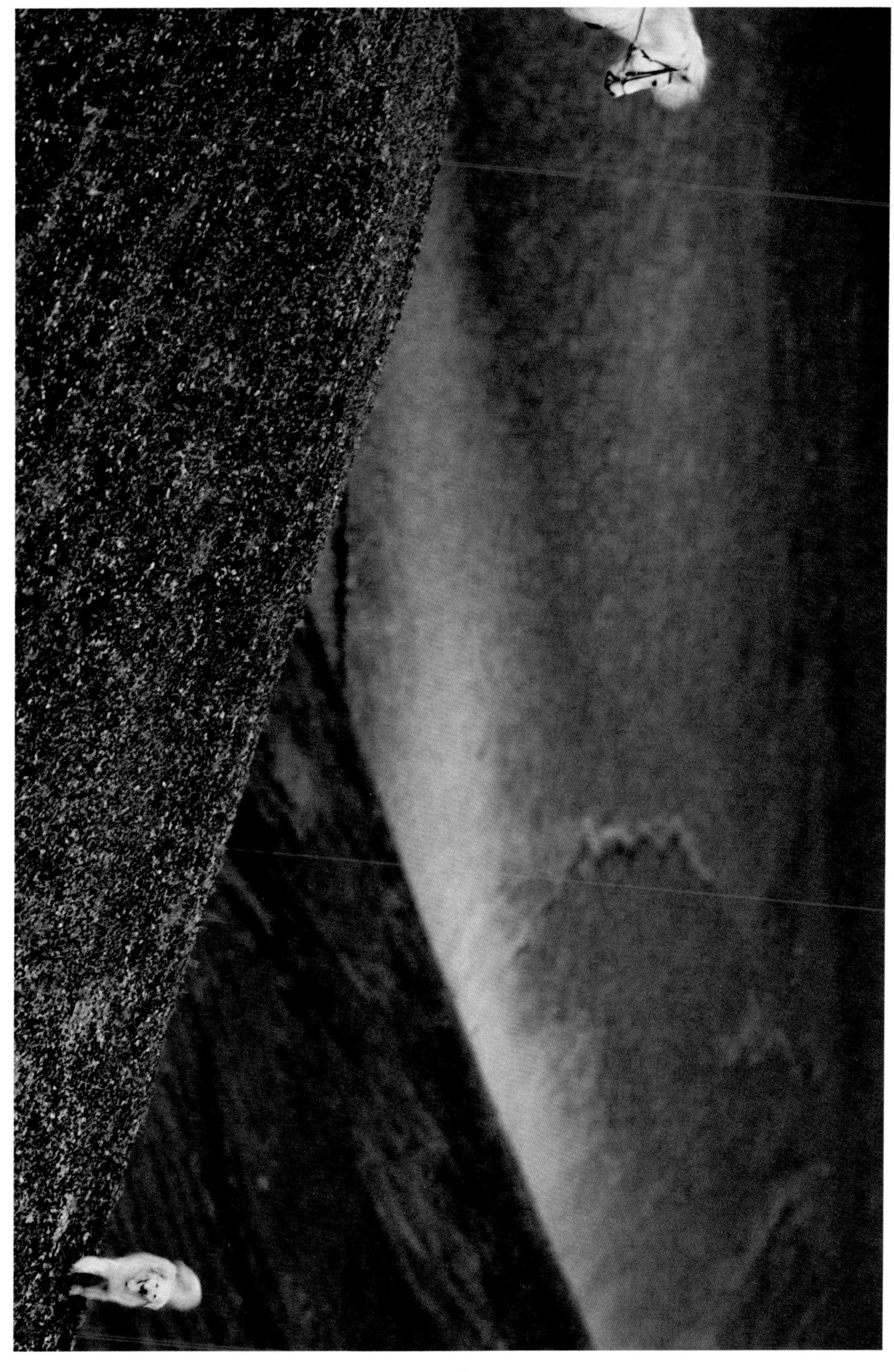

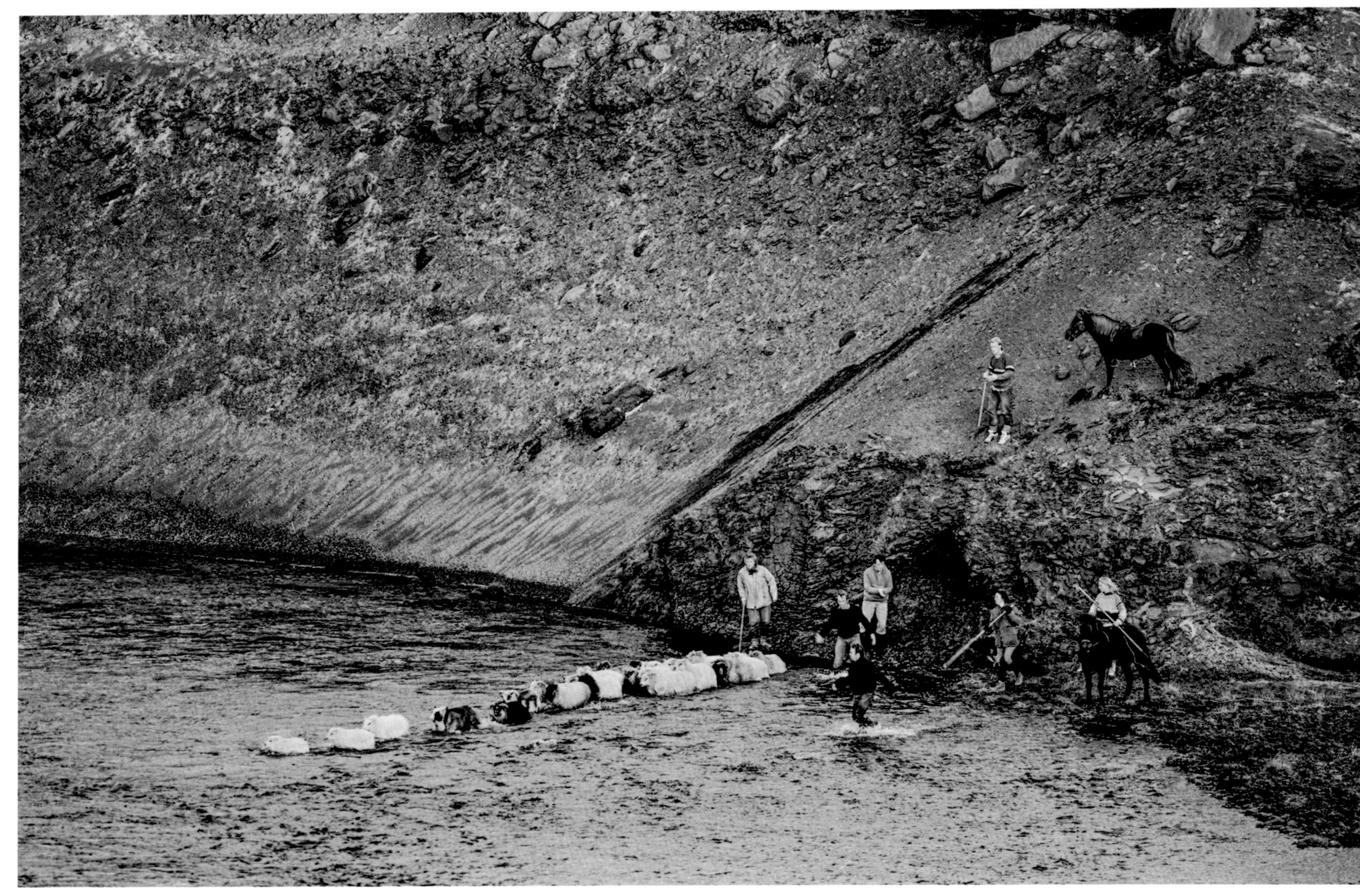

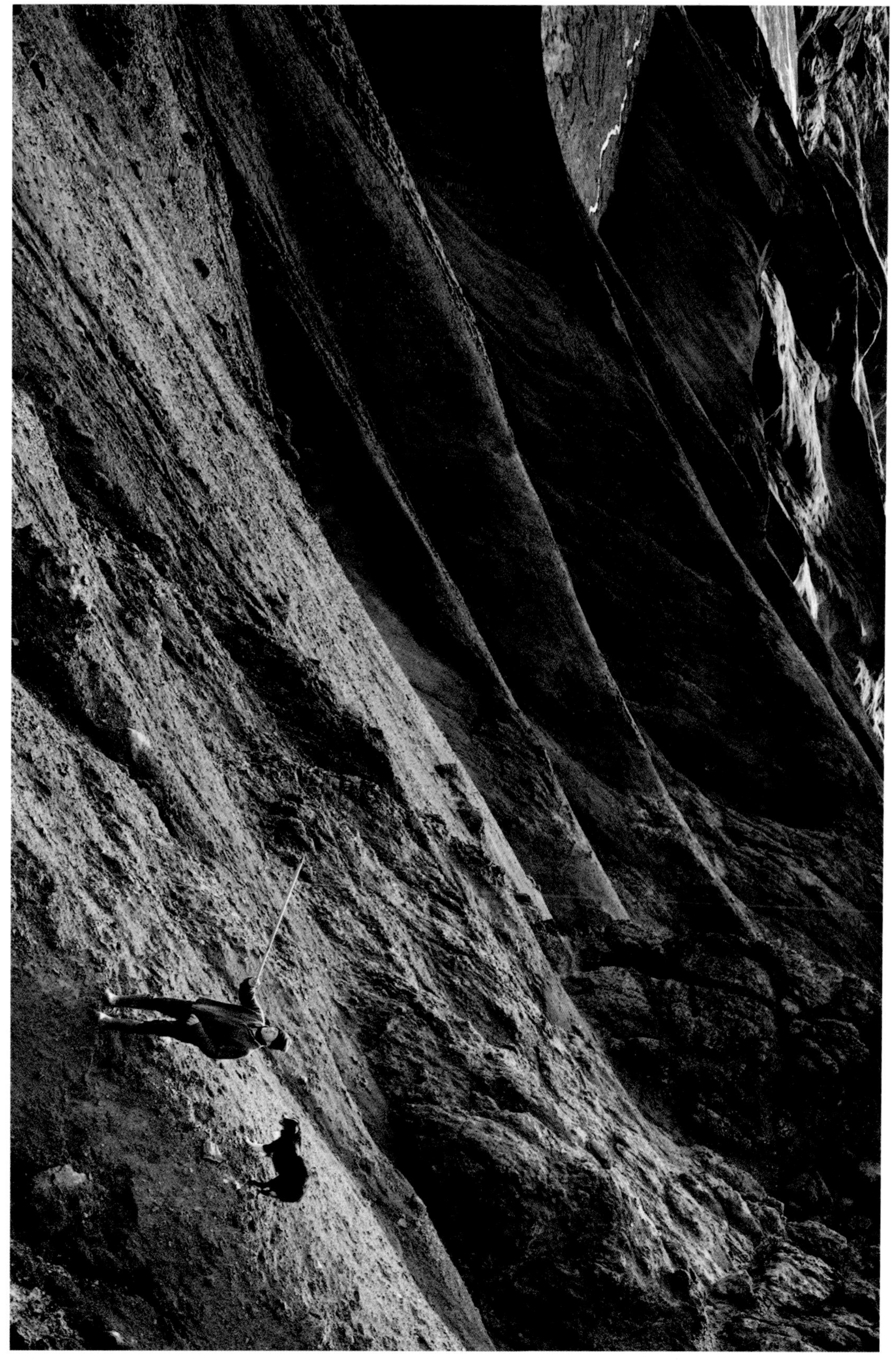

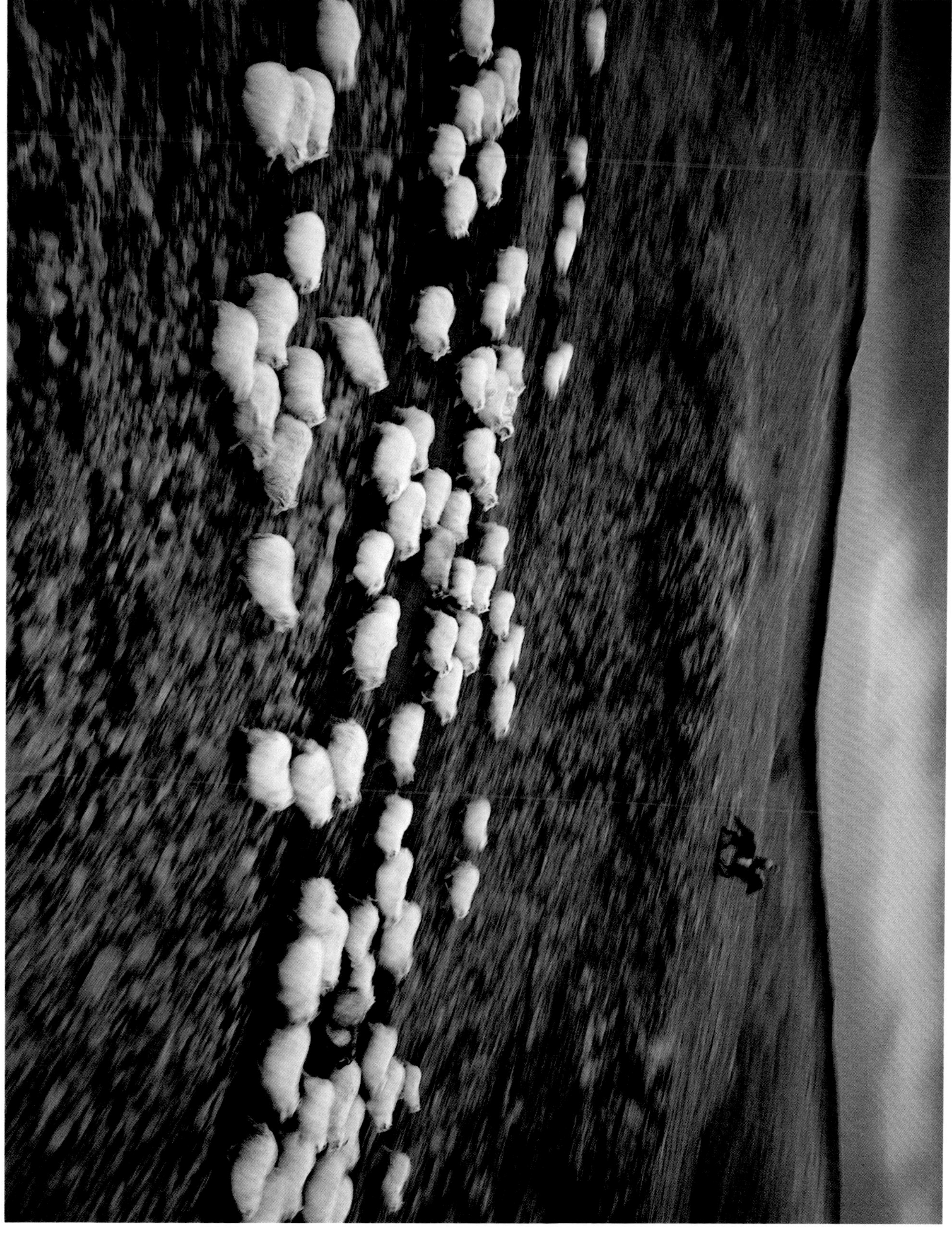

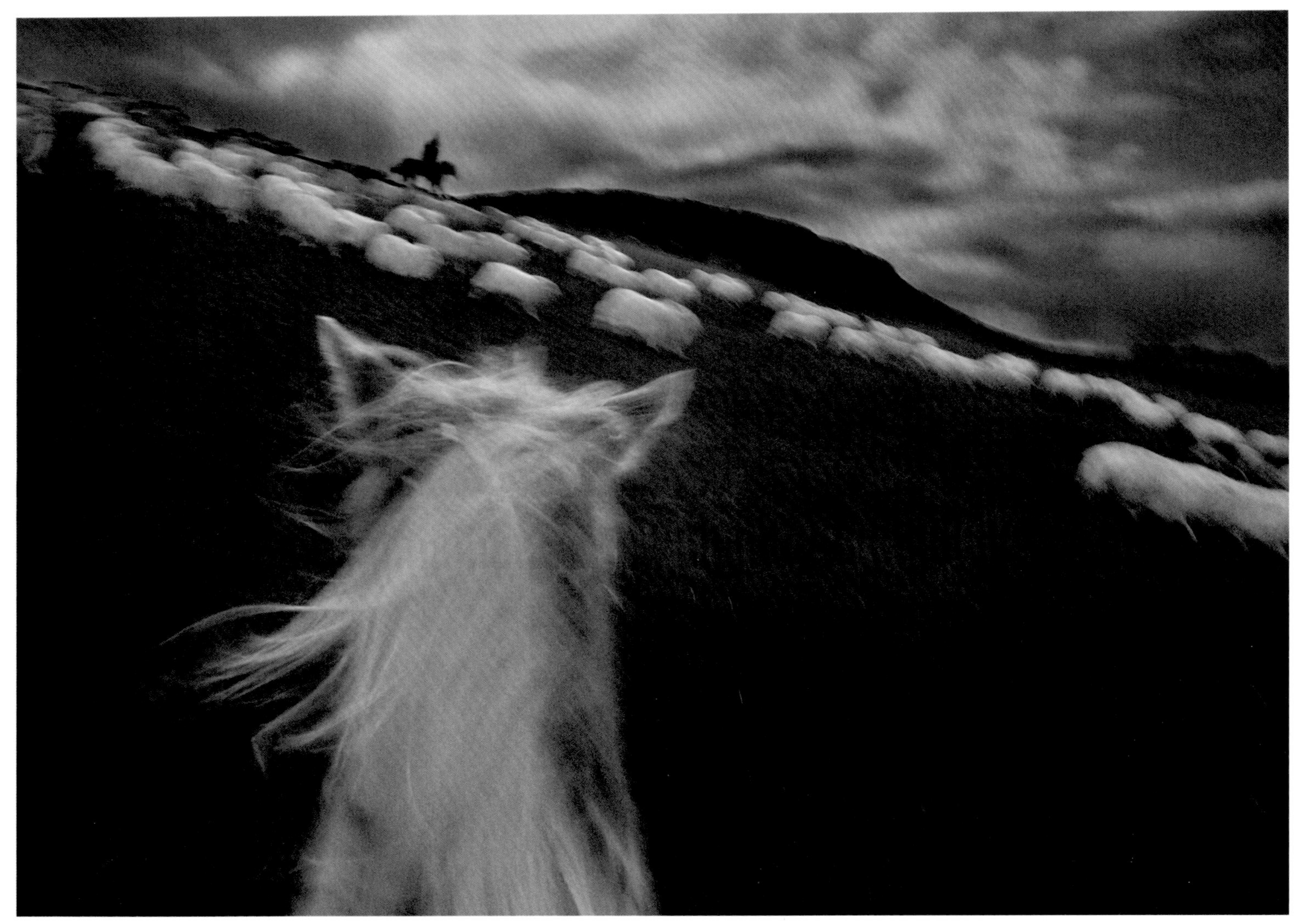

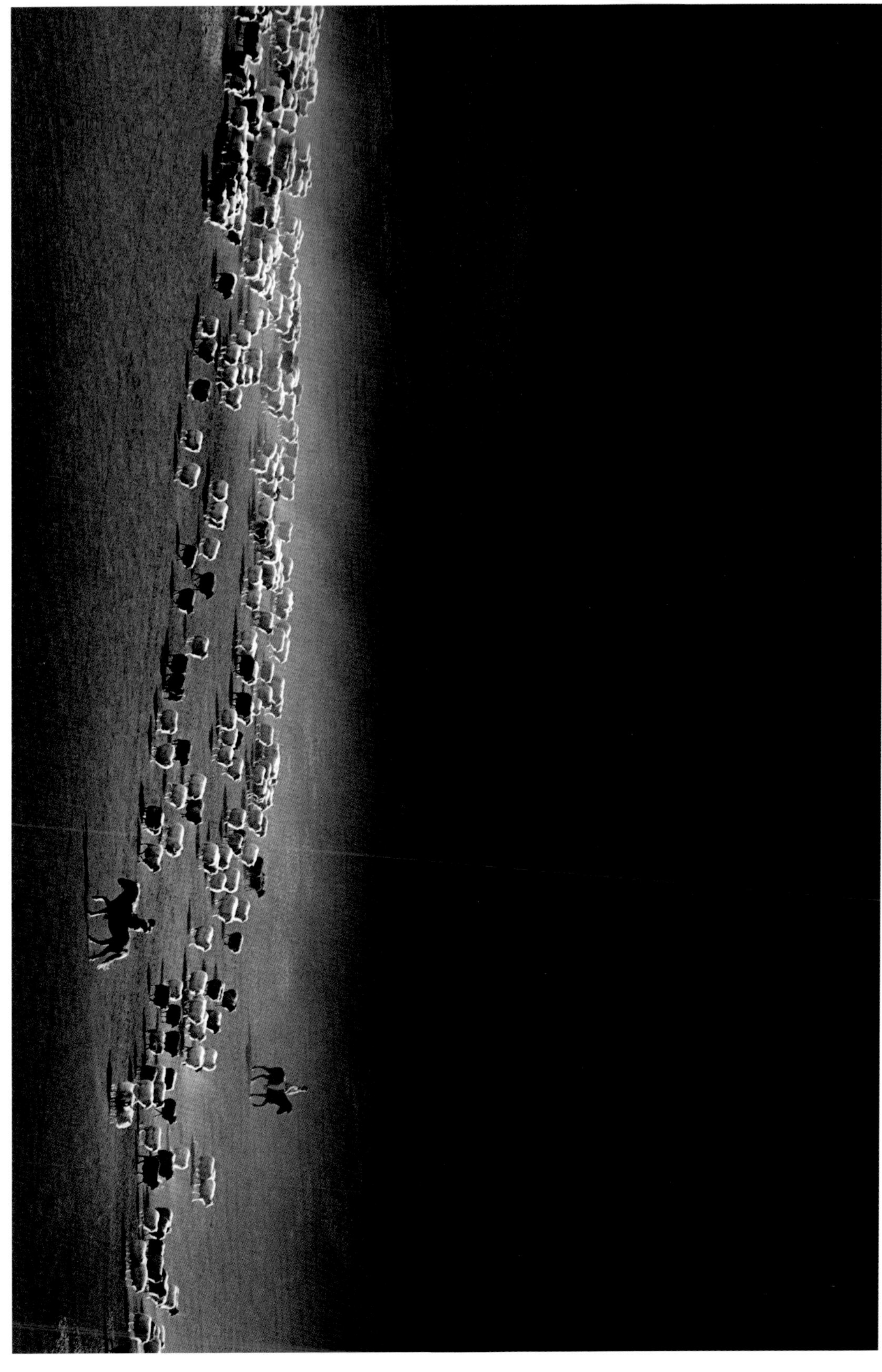

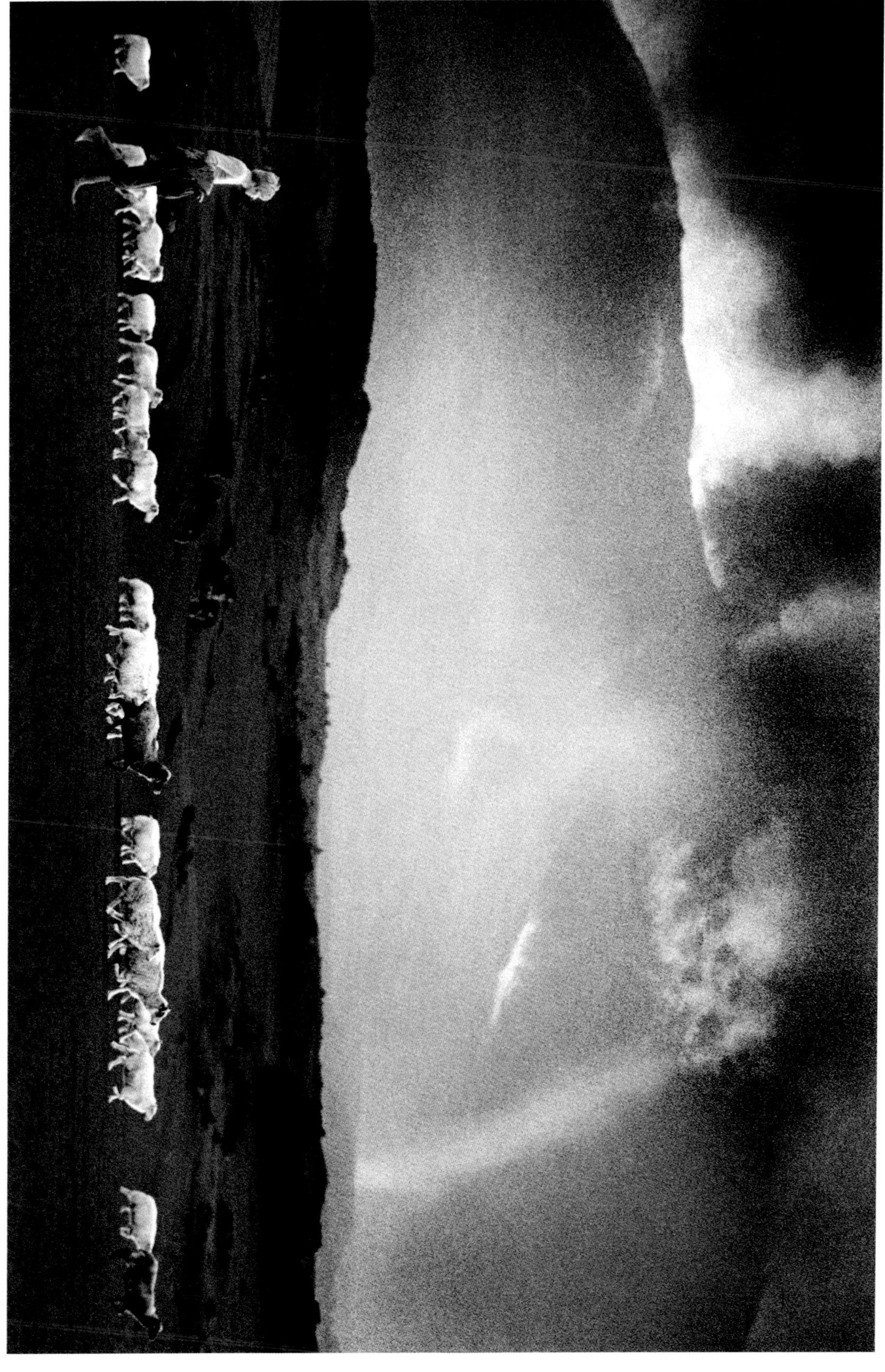

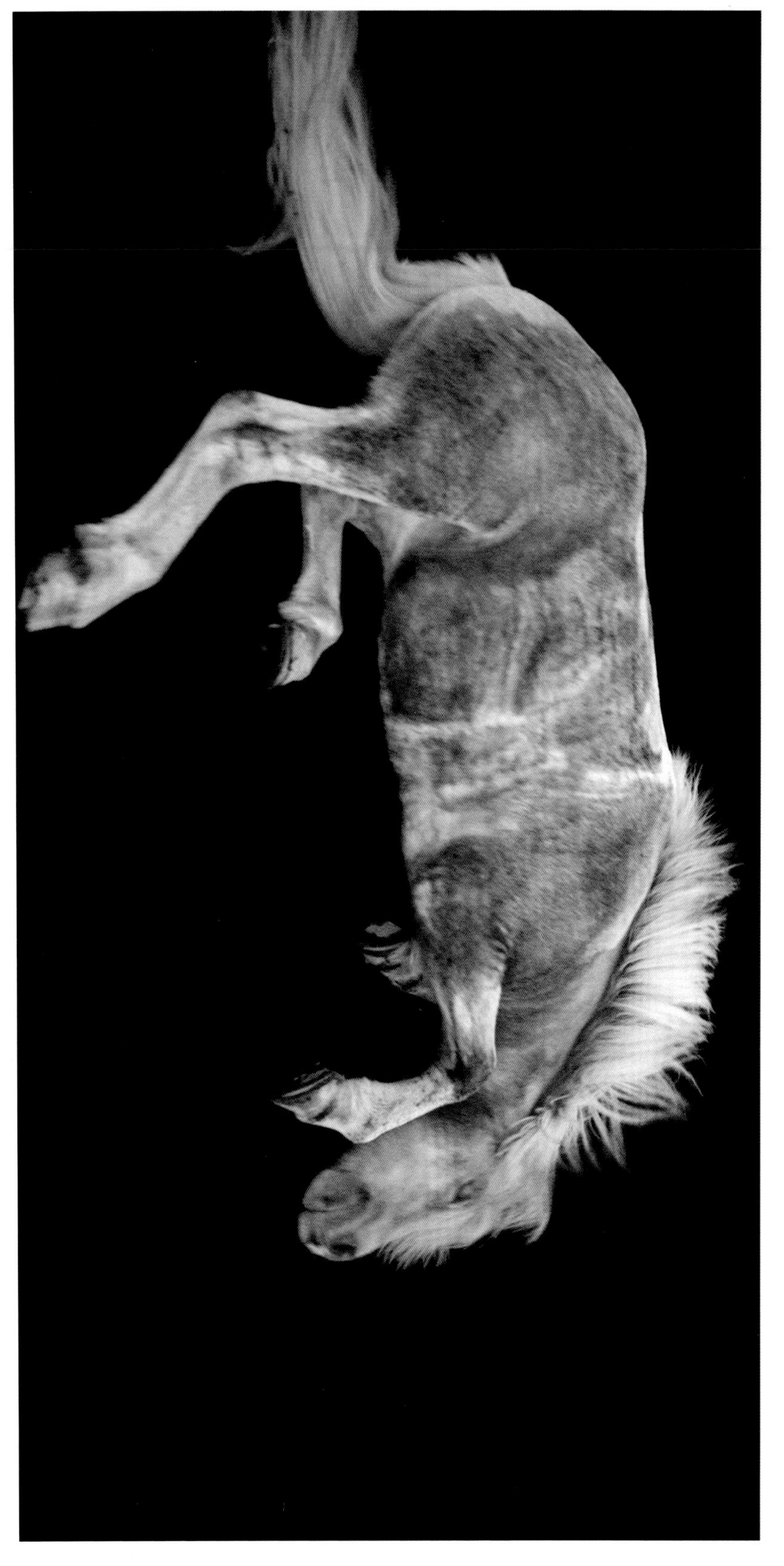

IV

Sorting

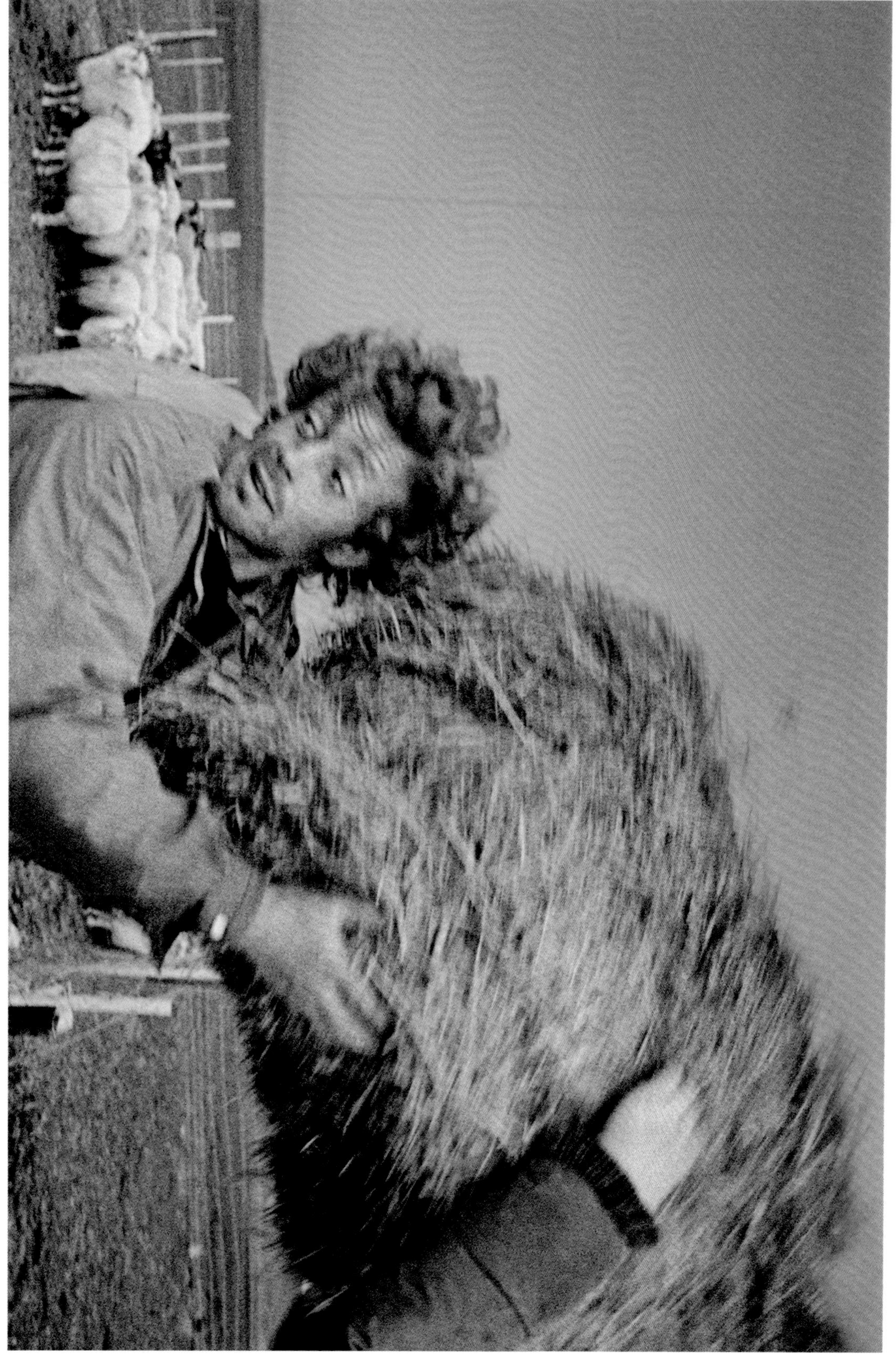

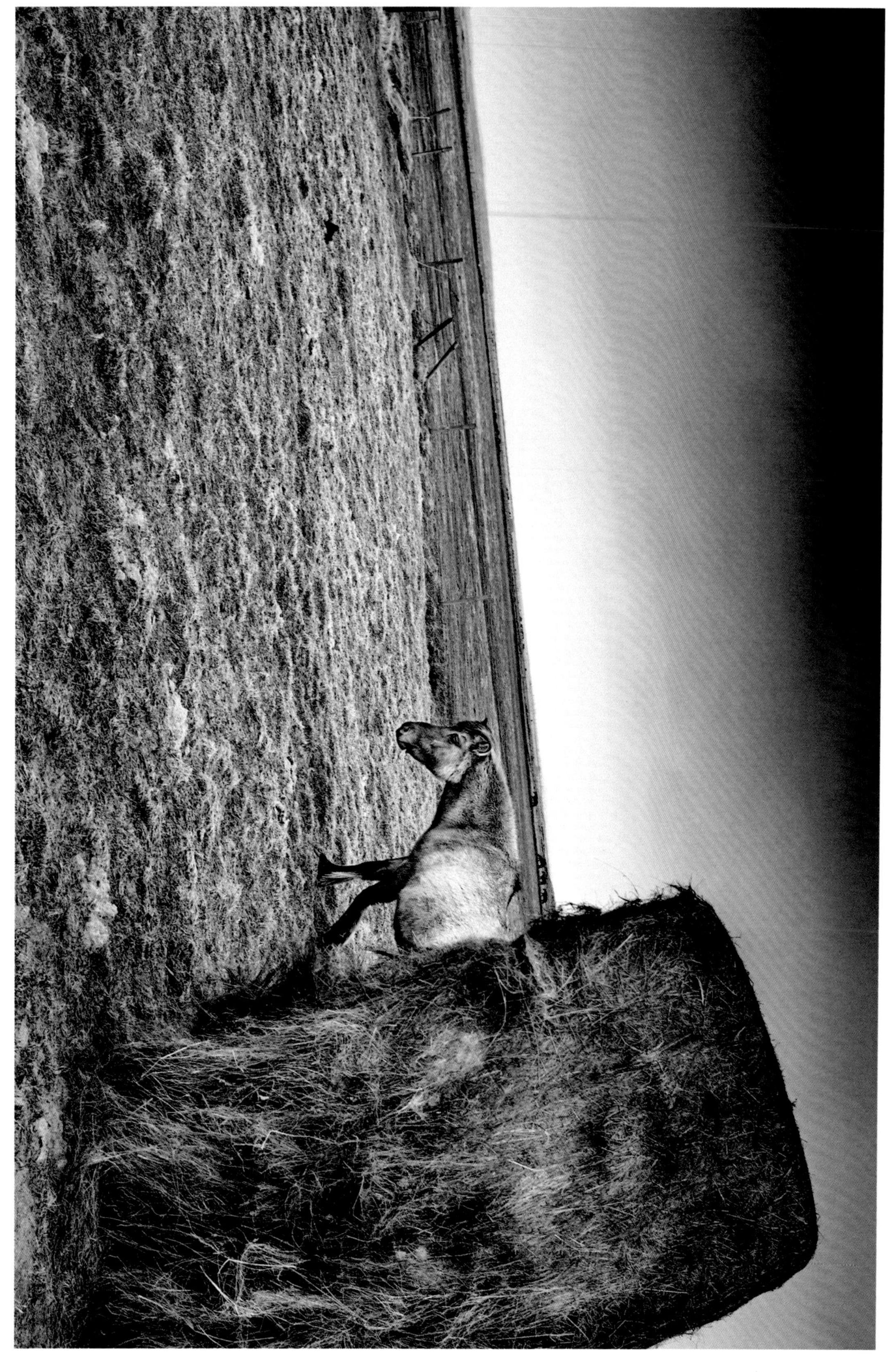

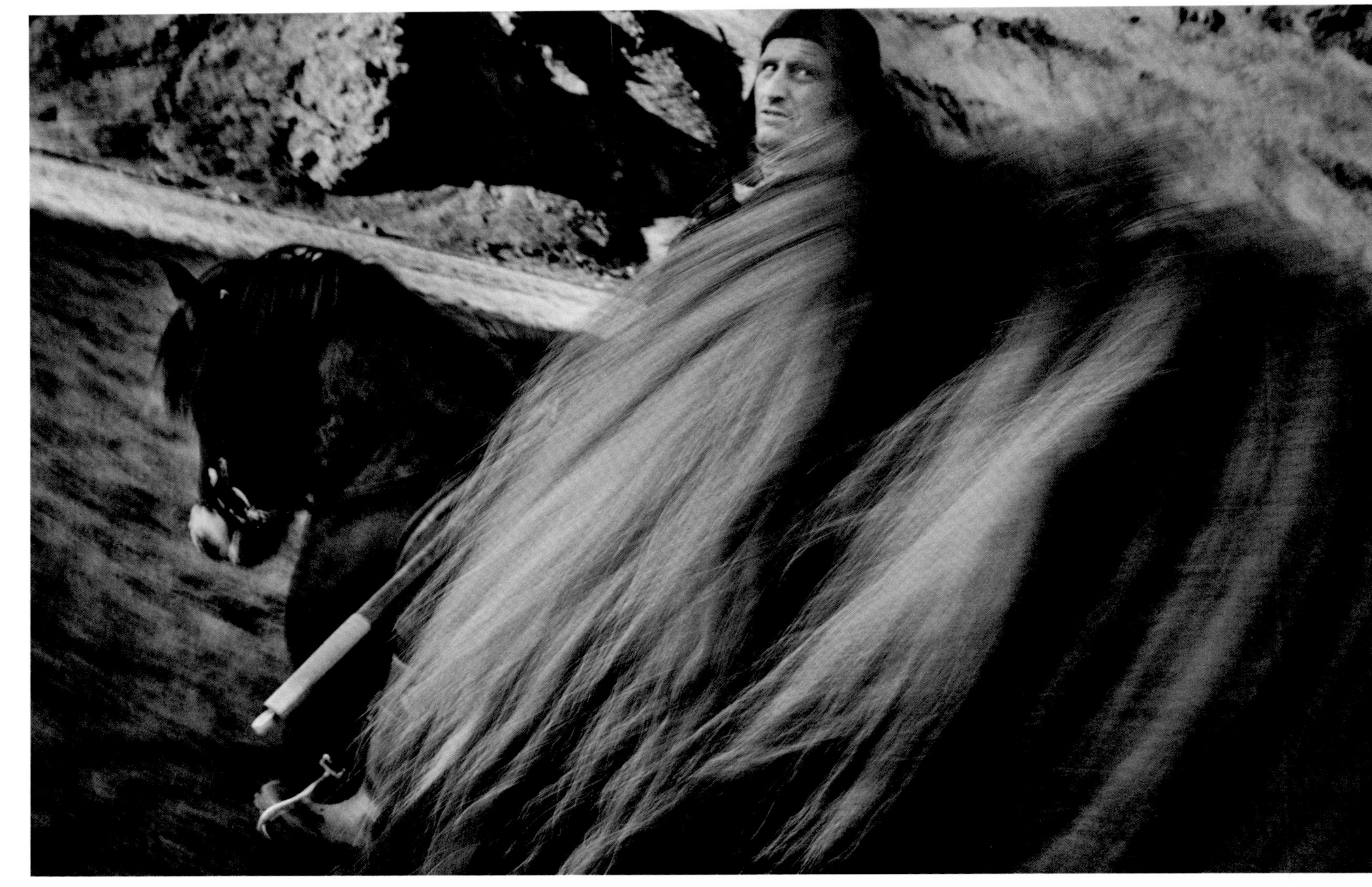

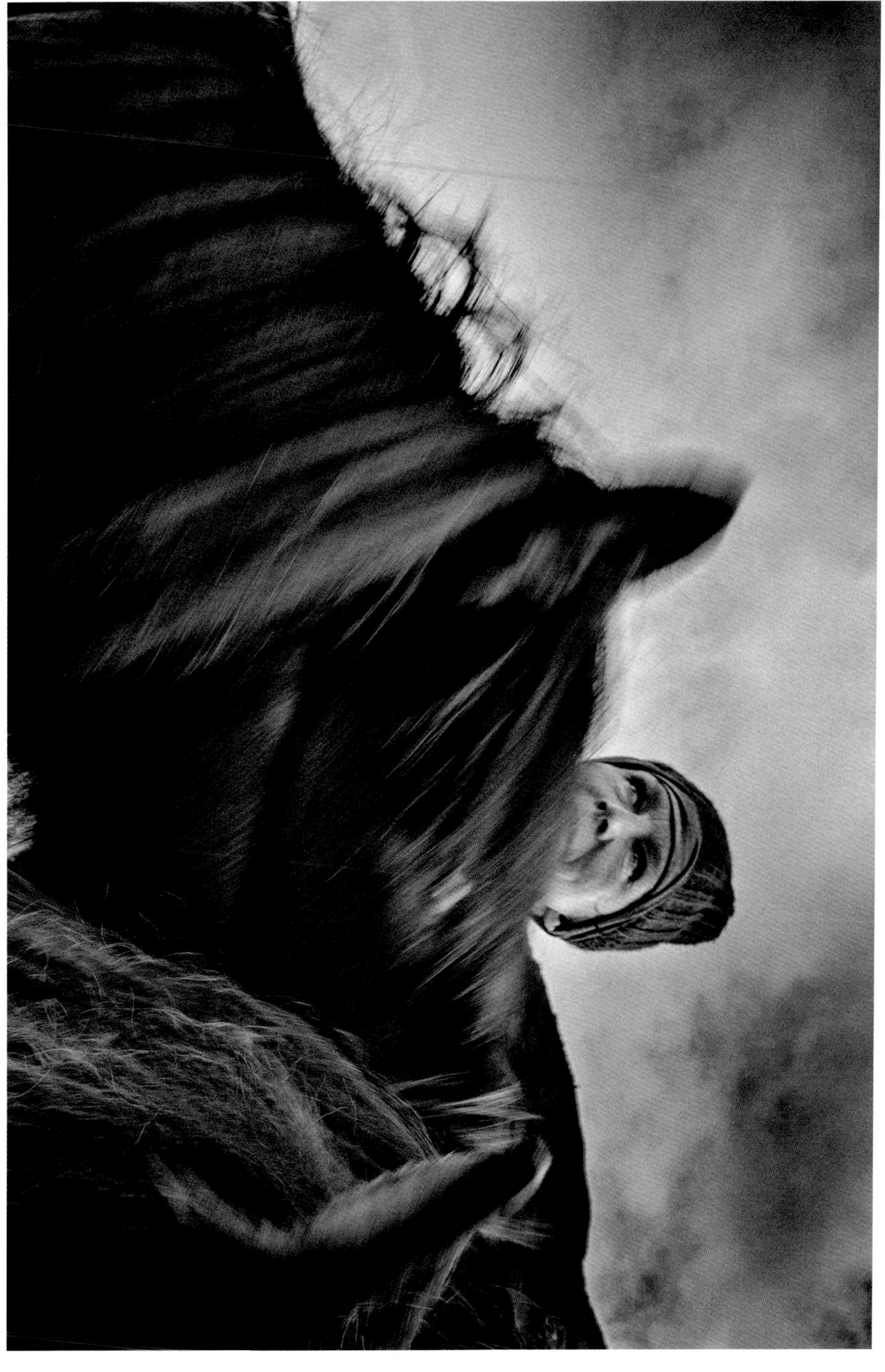

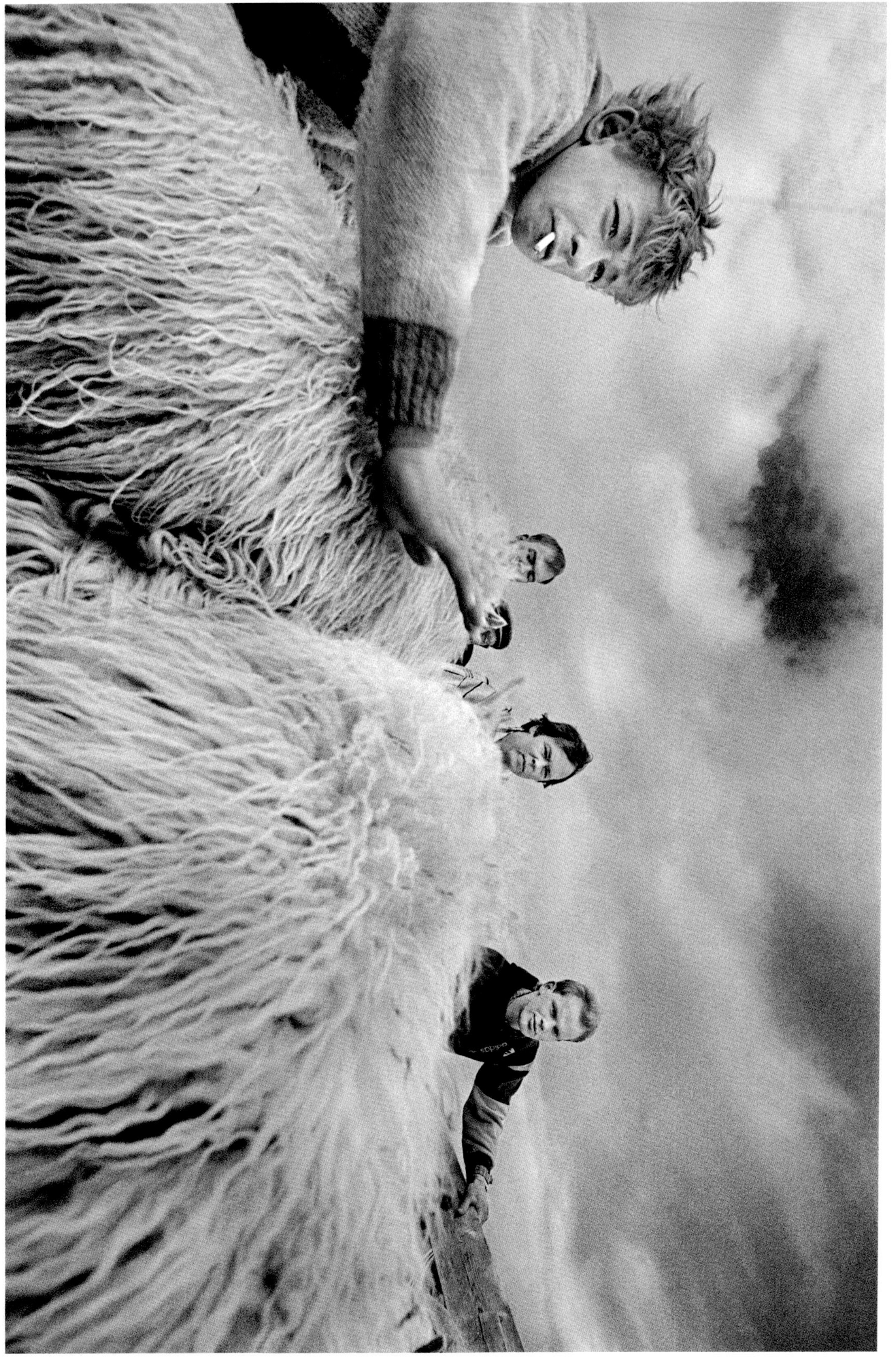

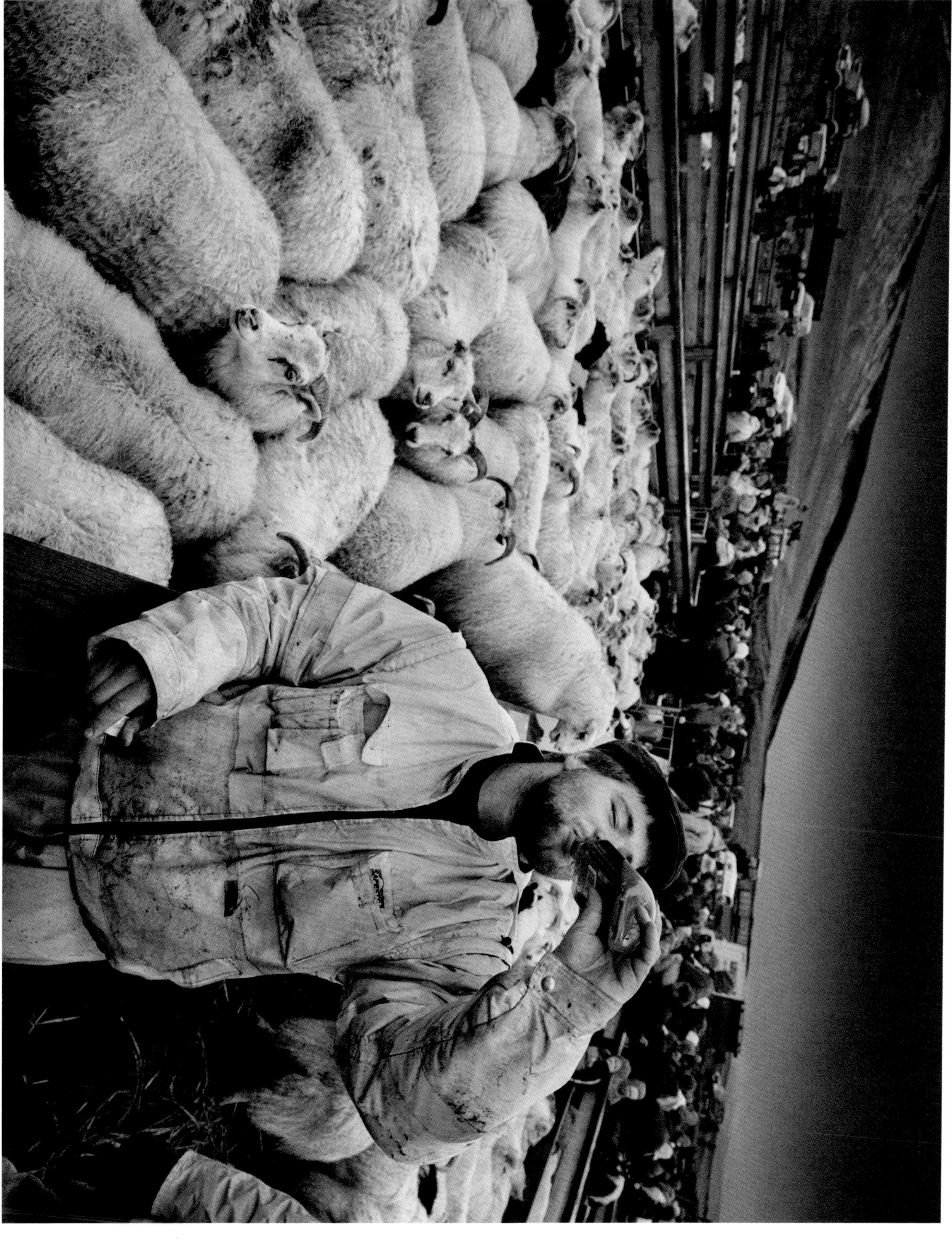

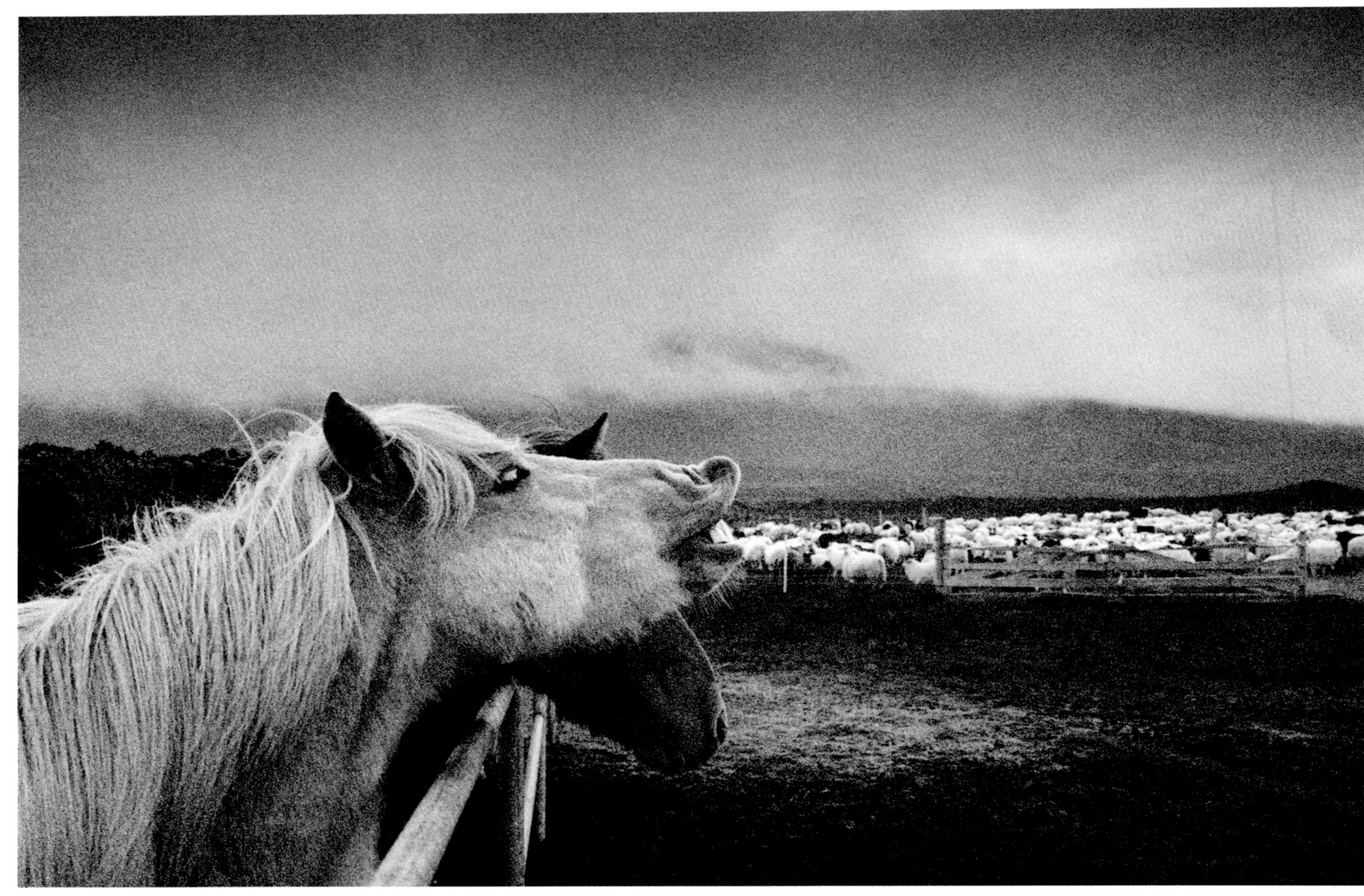

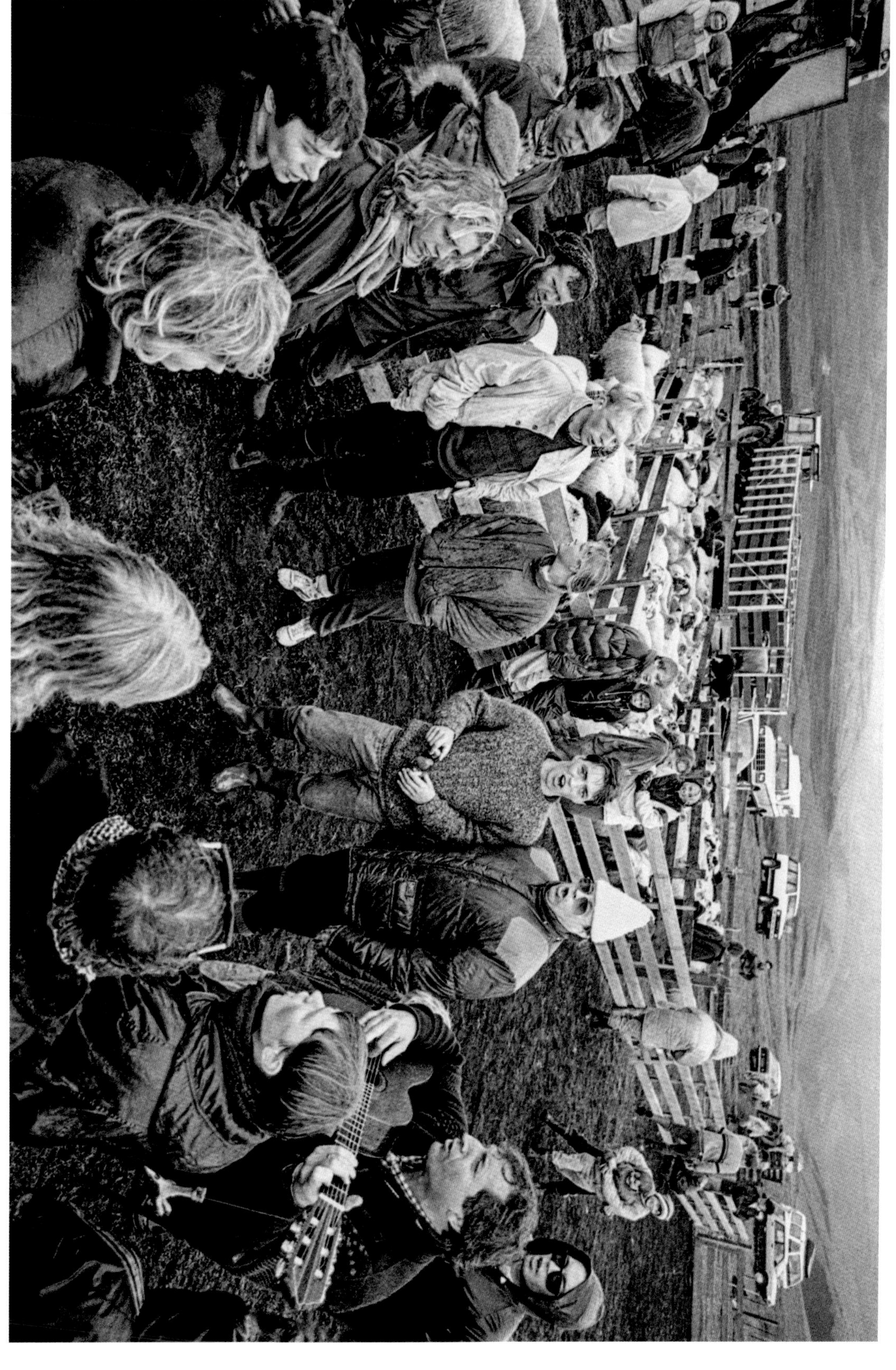

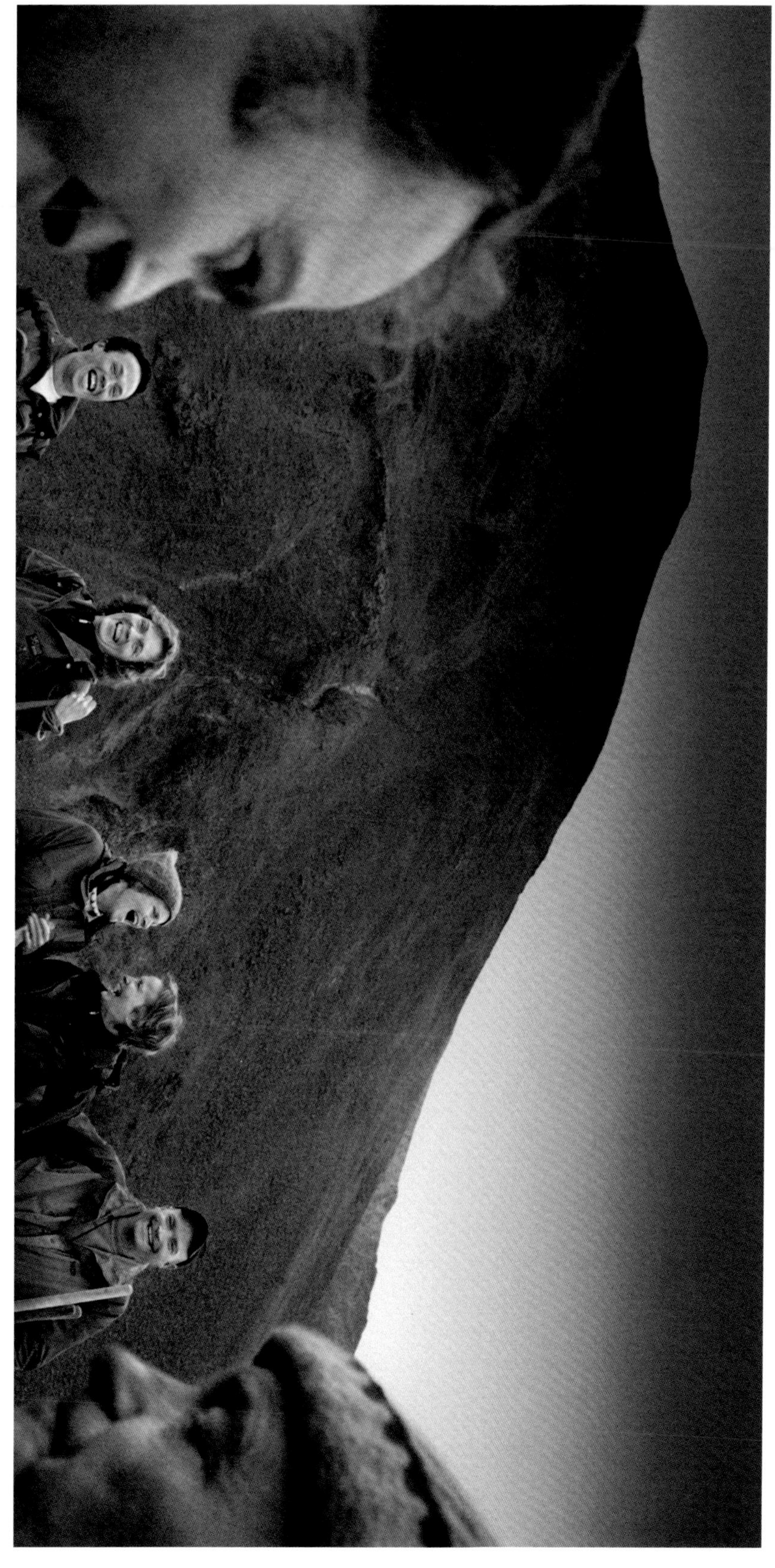

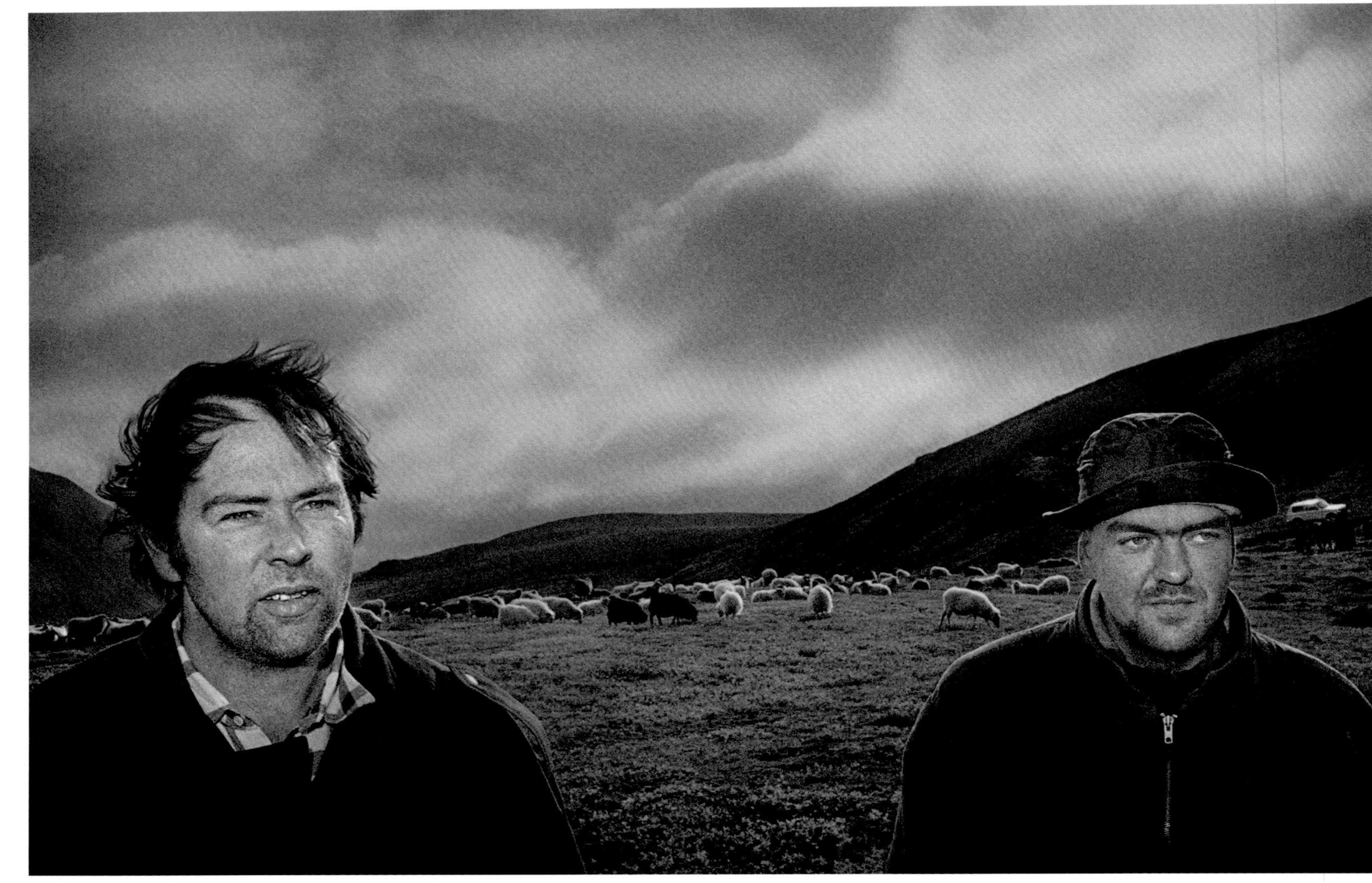

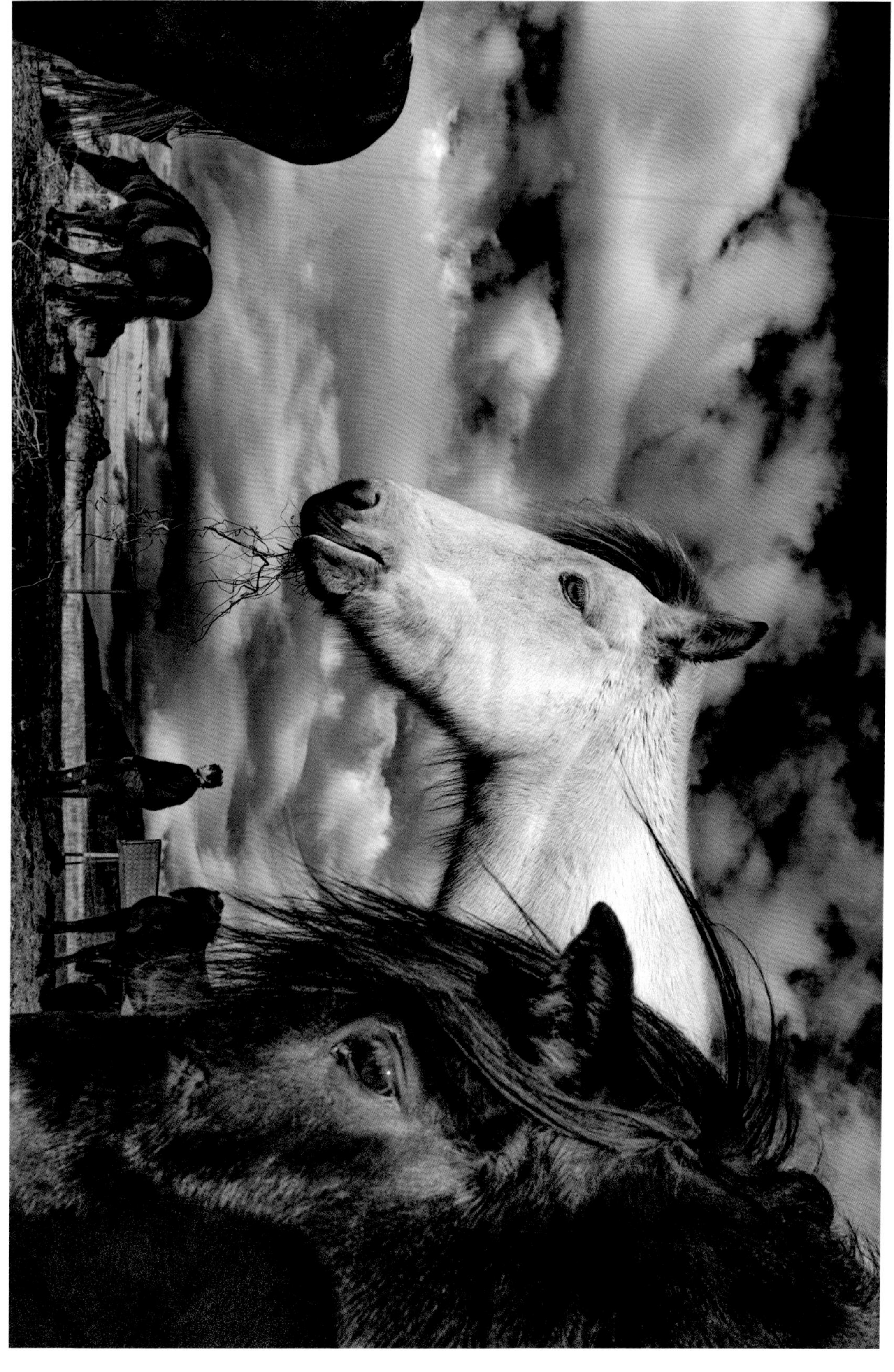

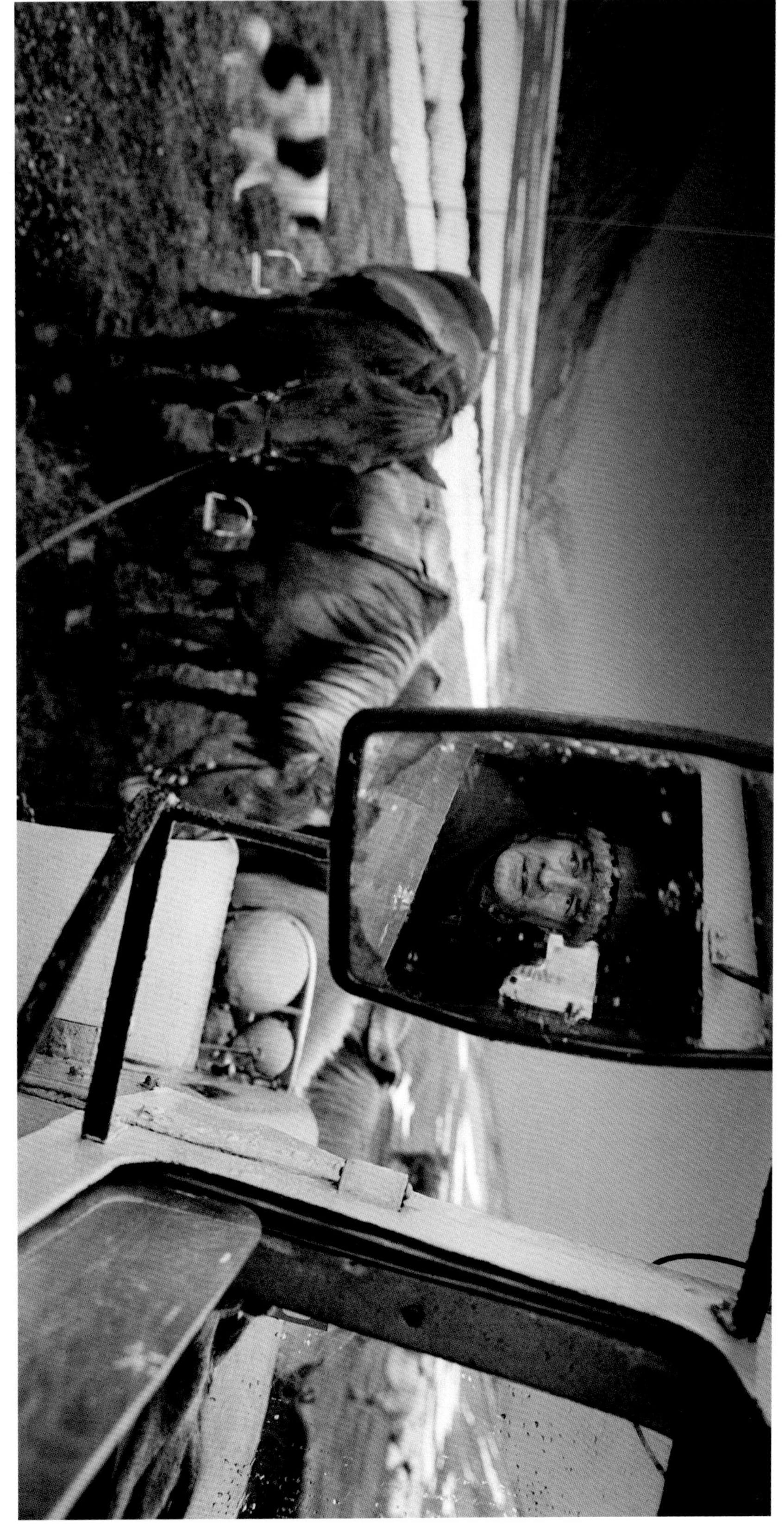

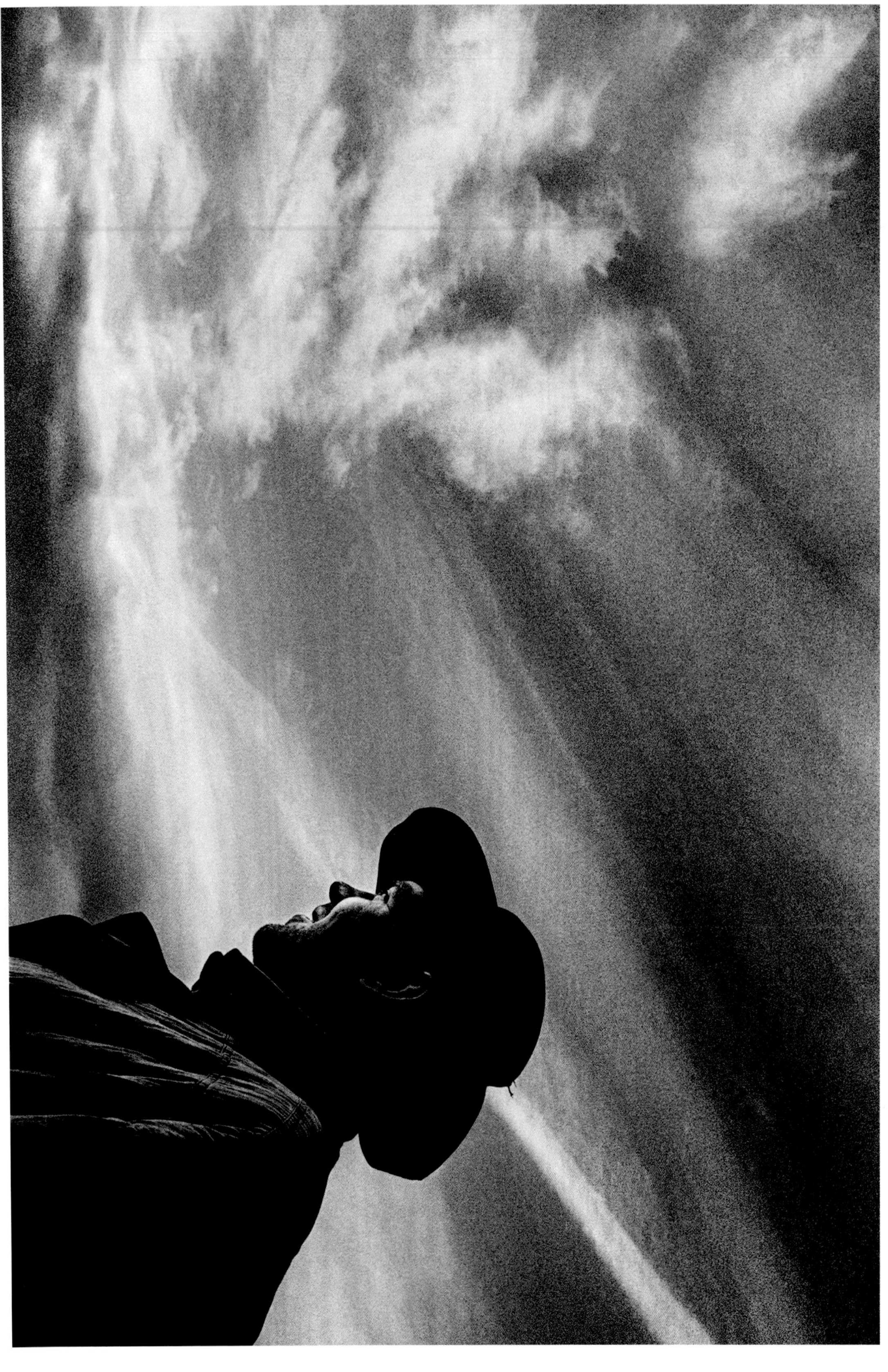

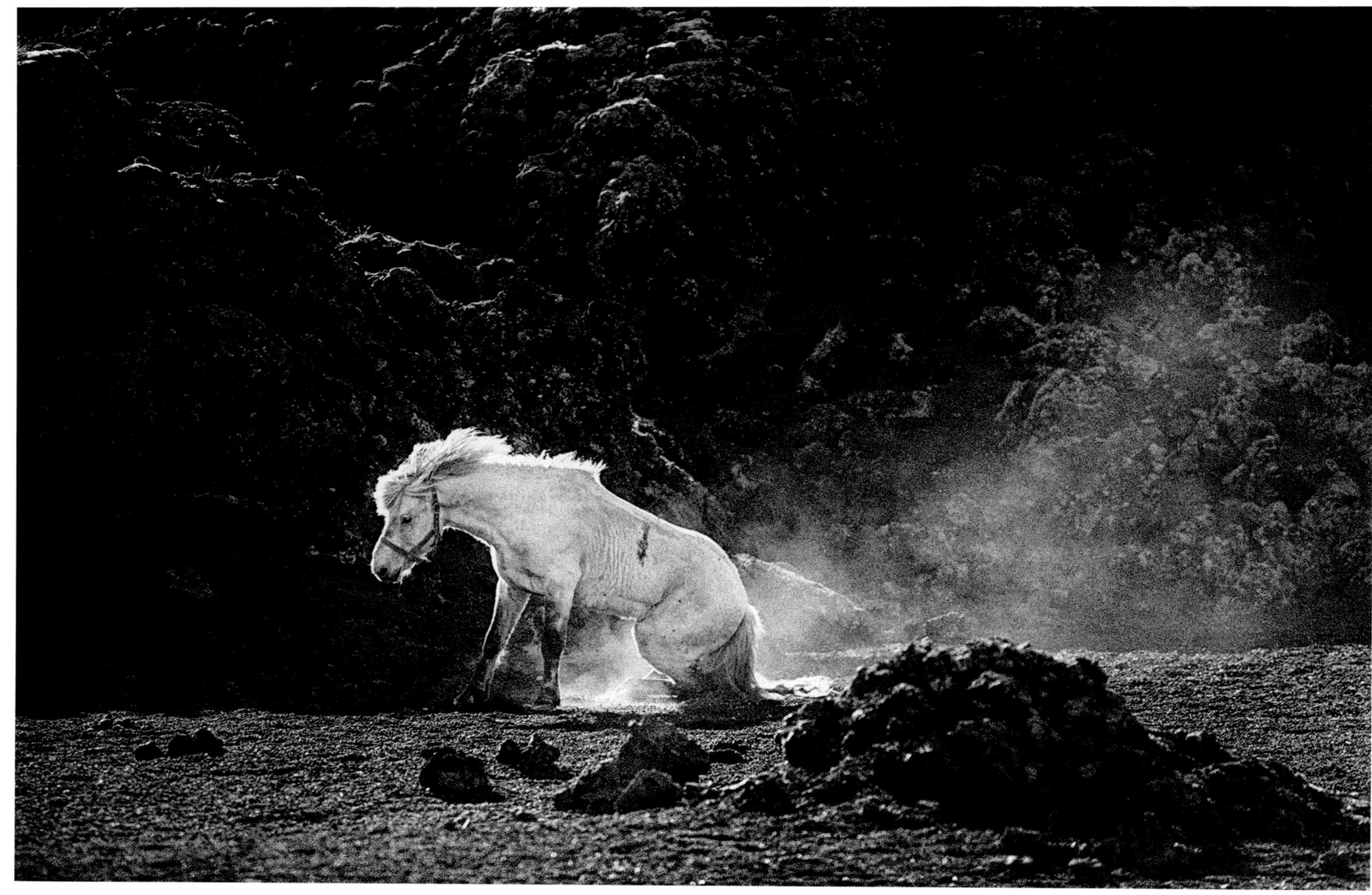

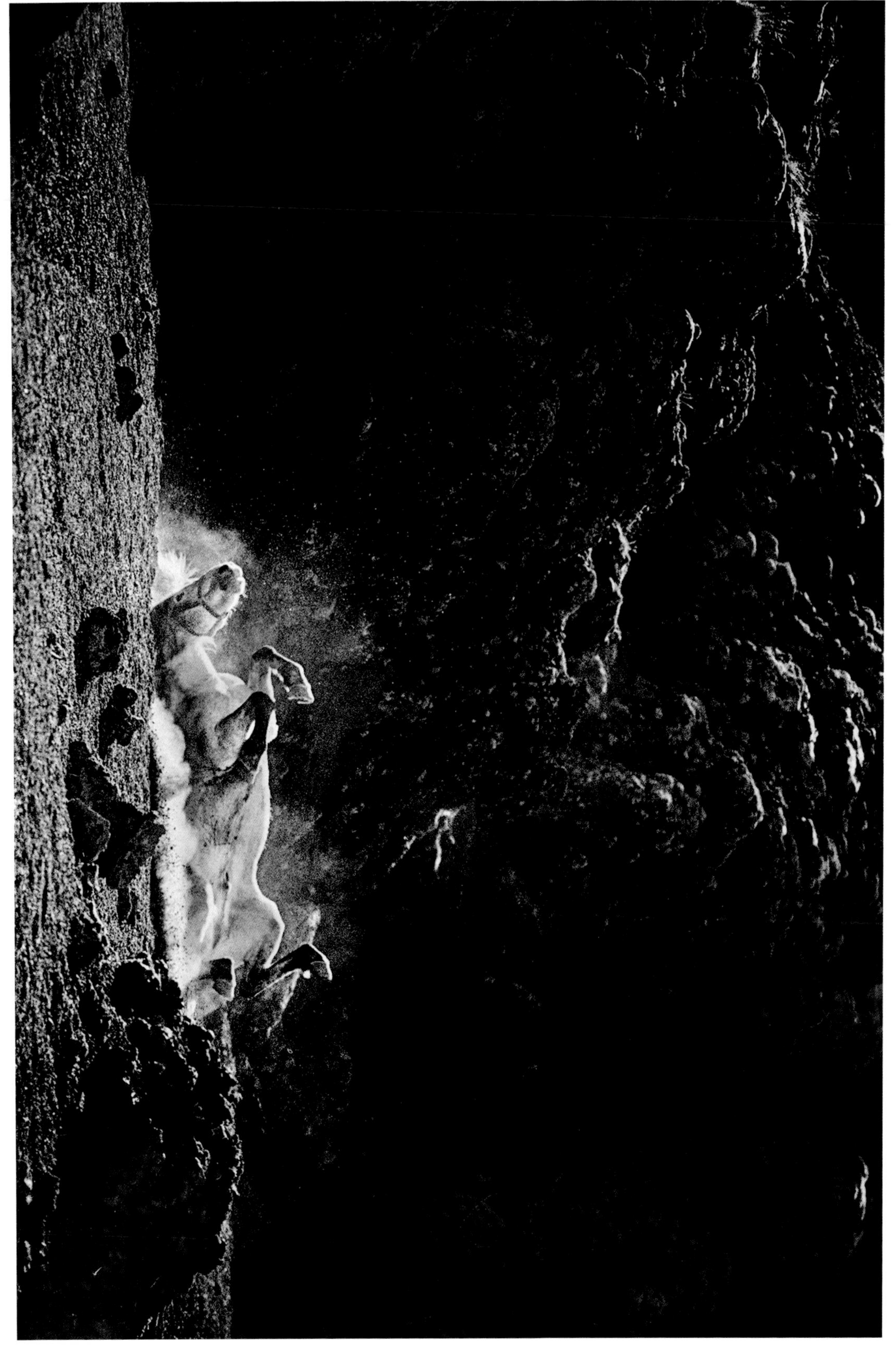

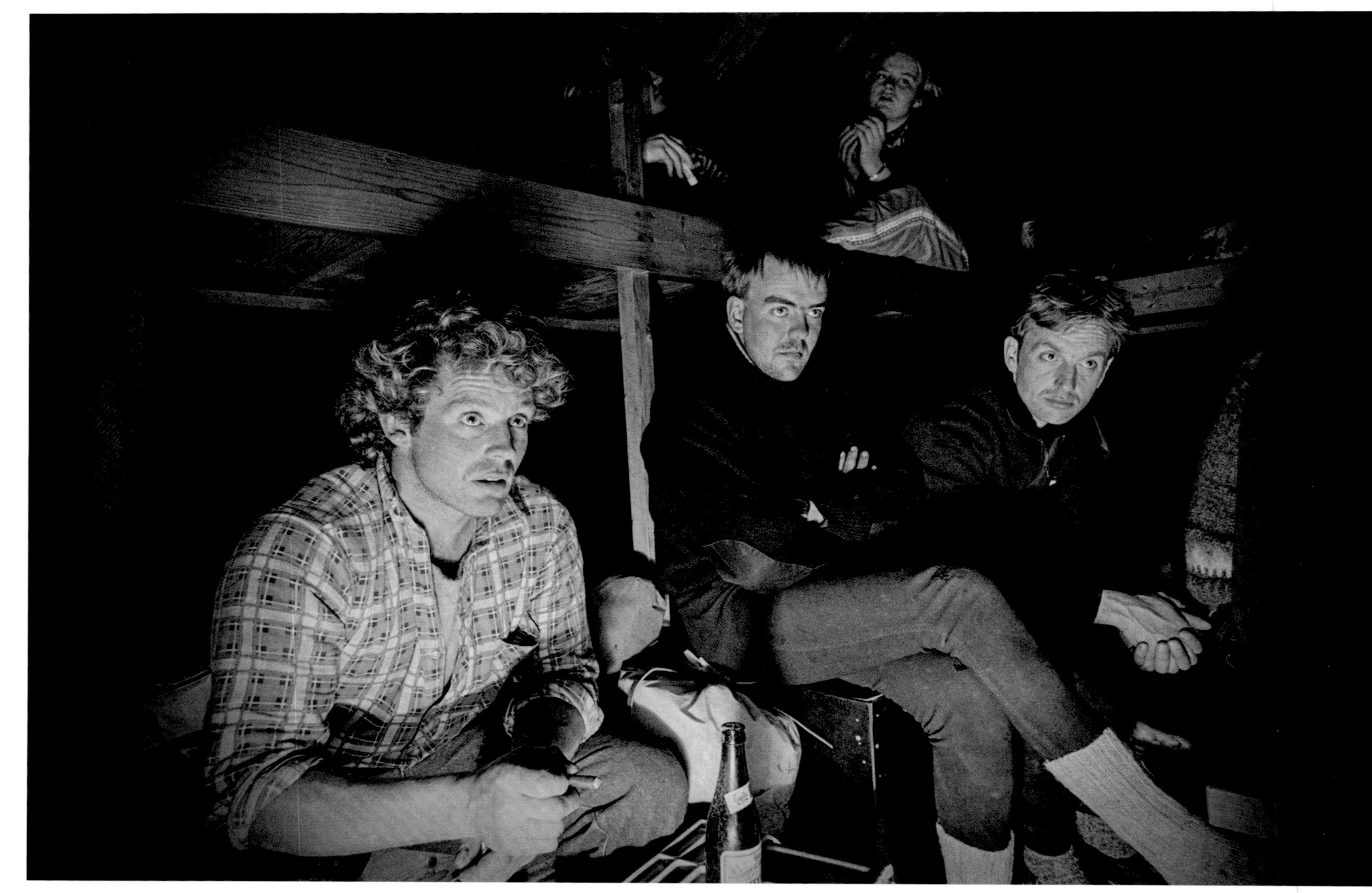

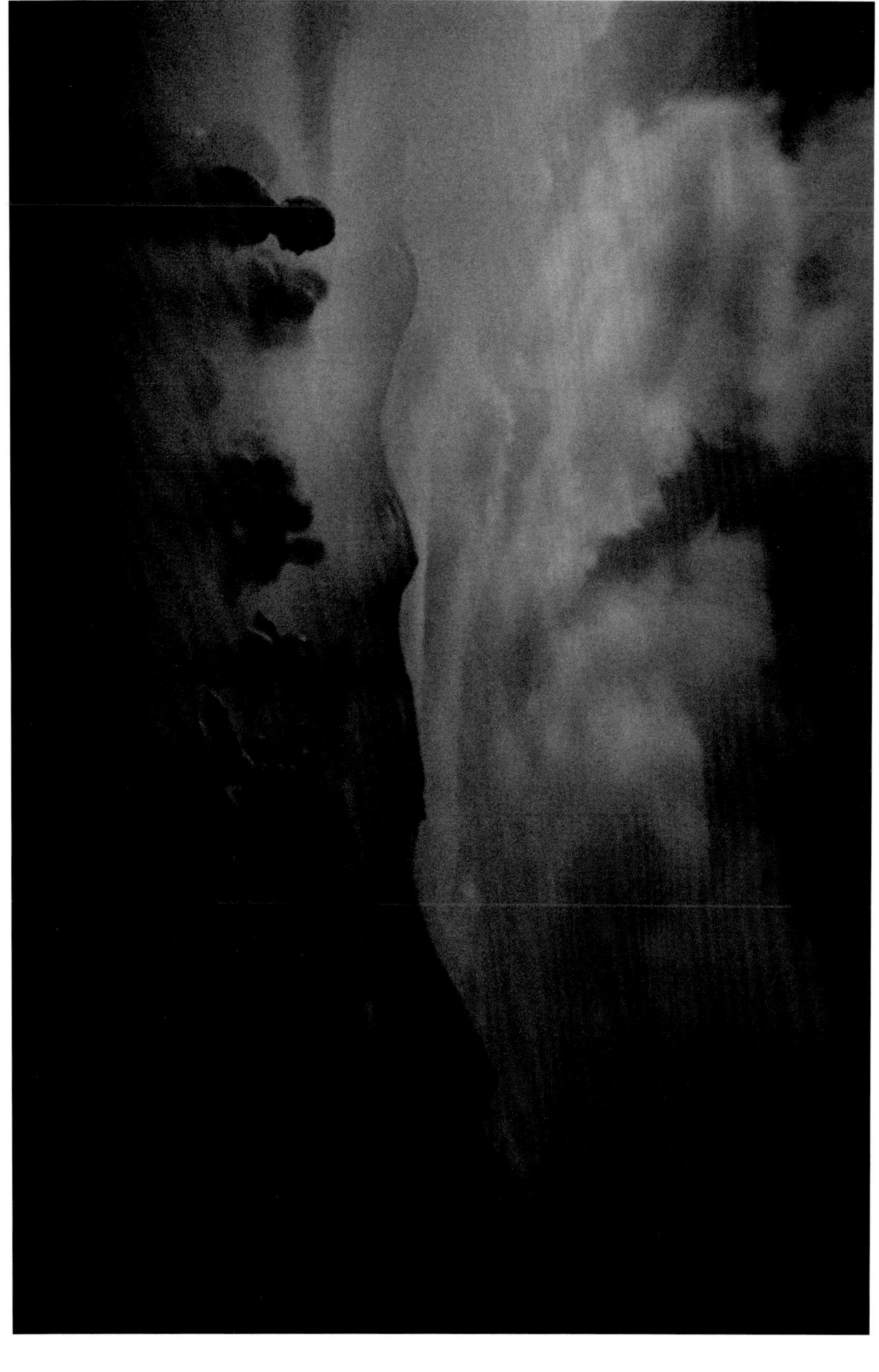

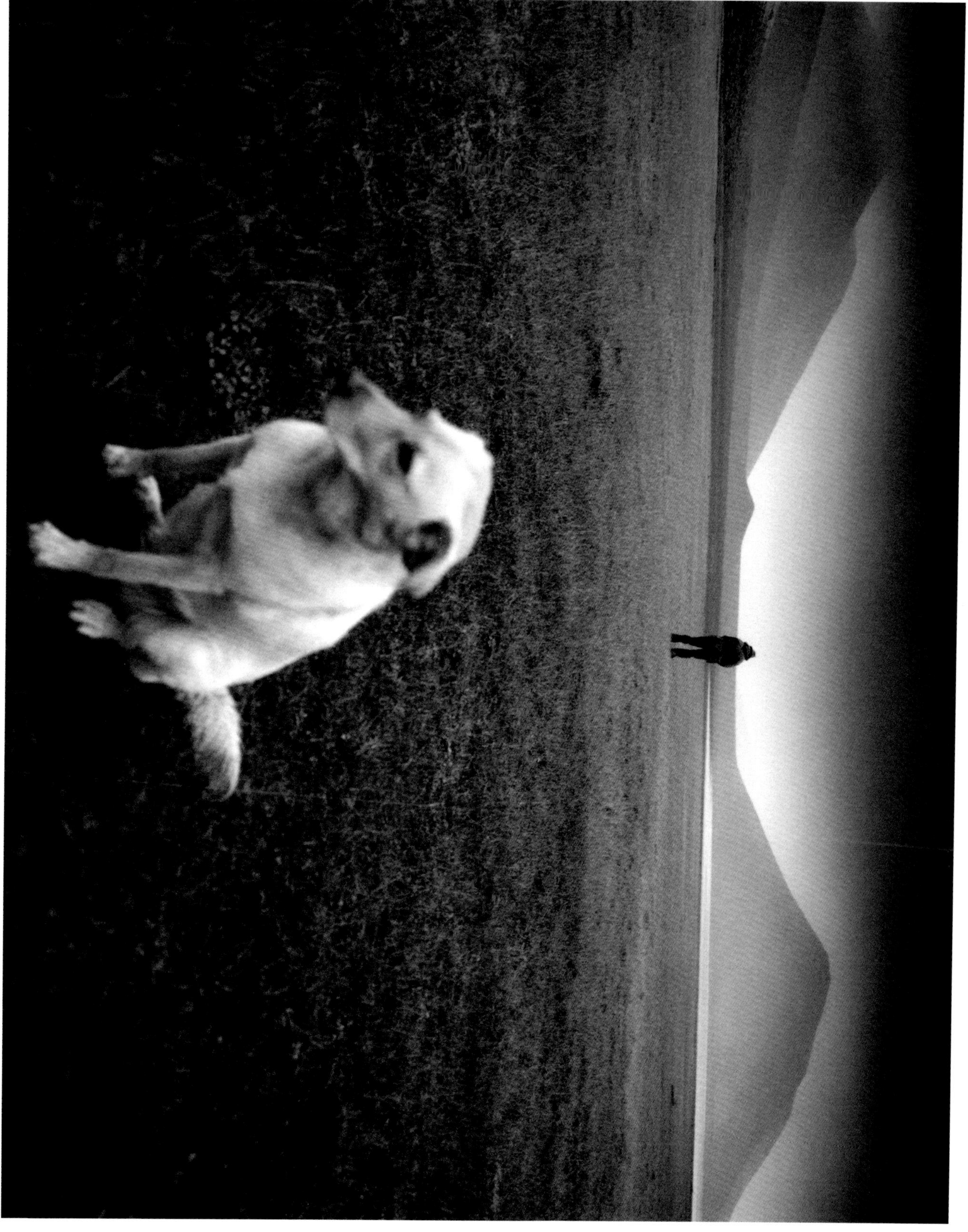

V

Last Search

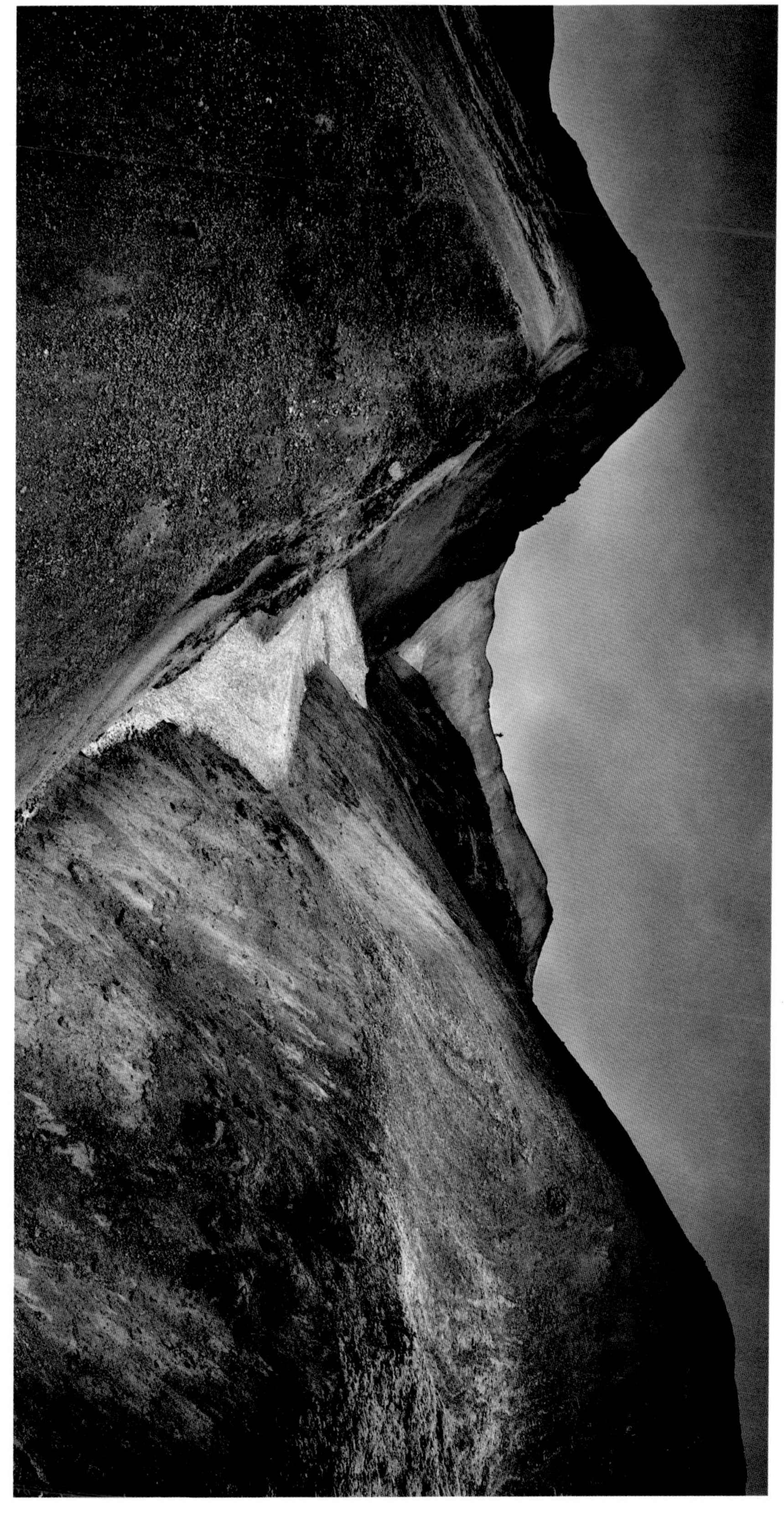

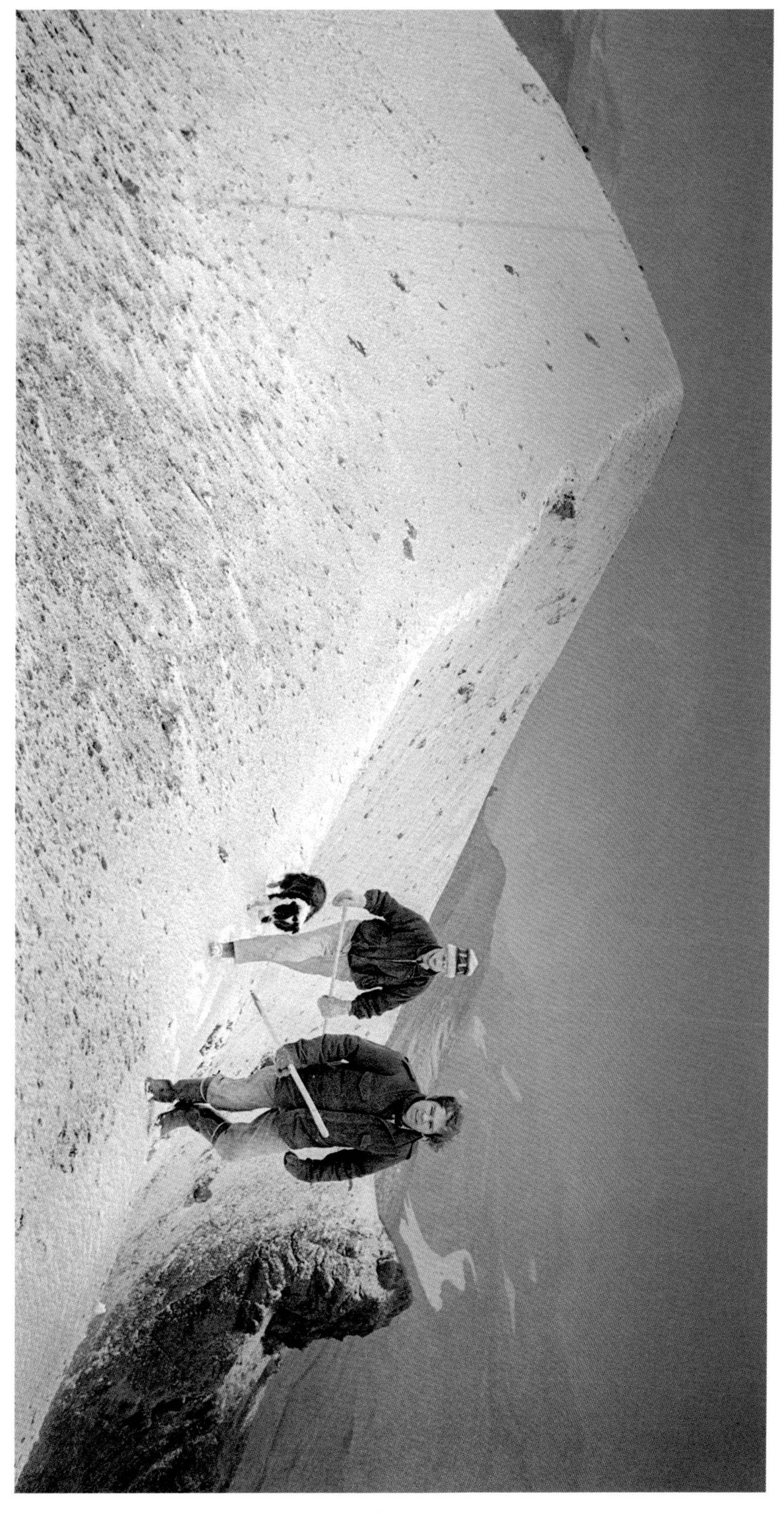

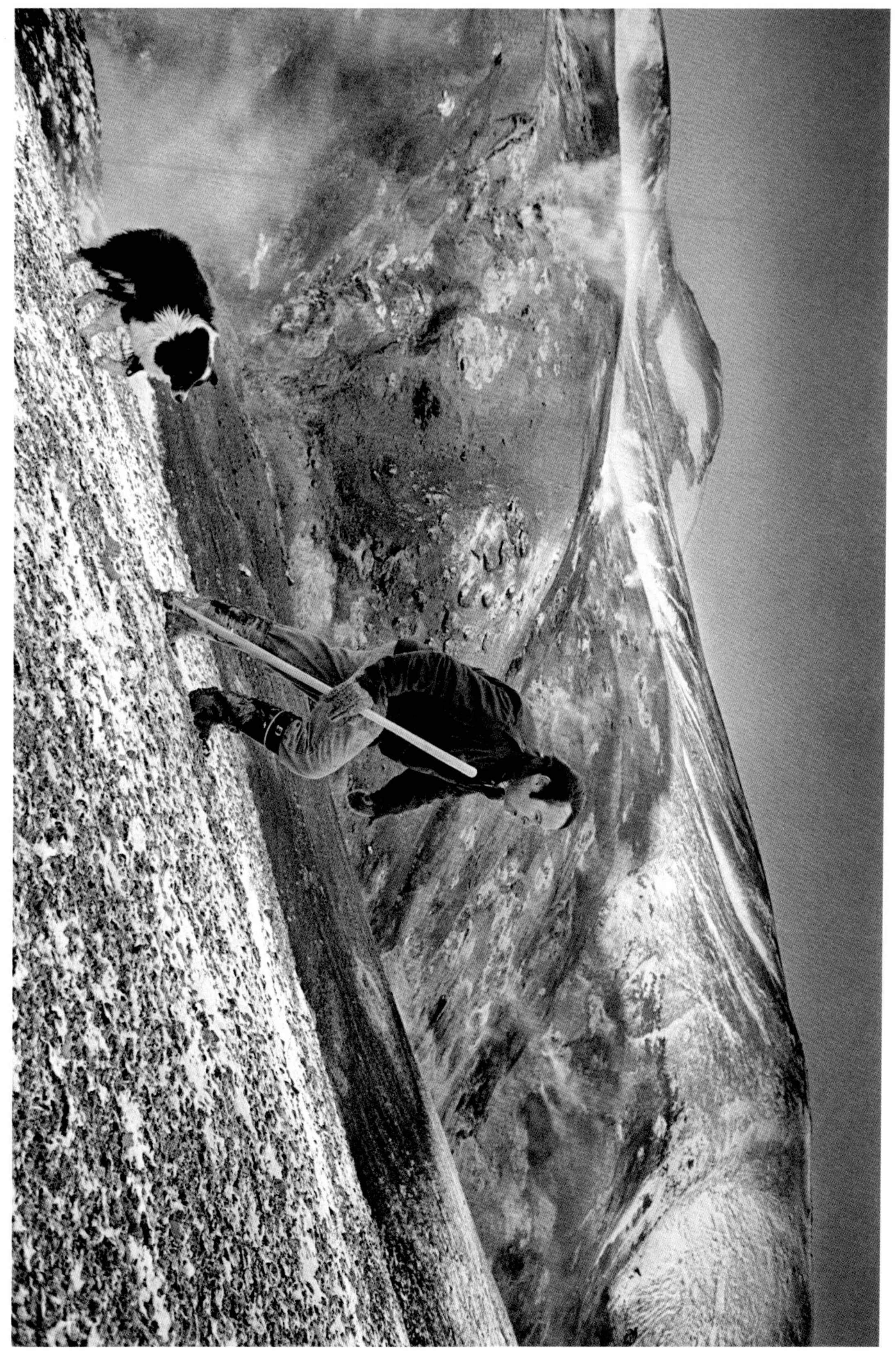

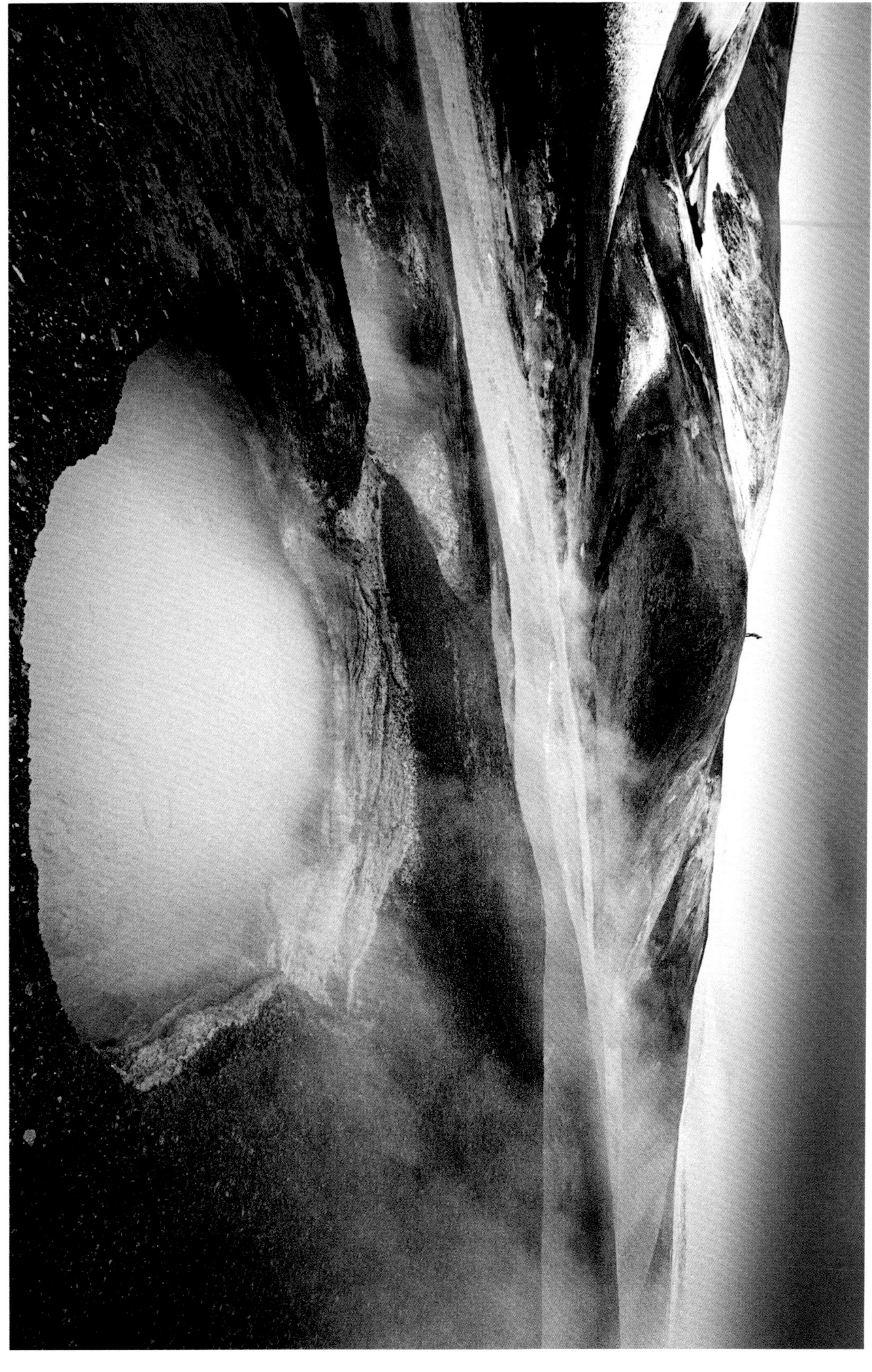

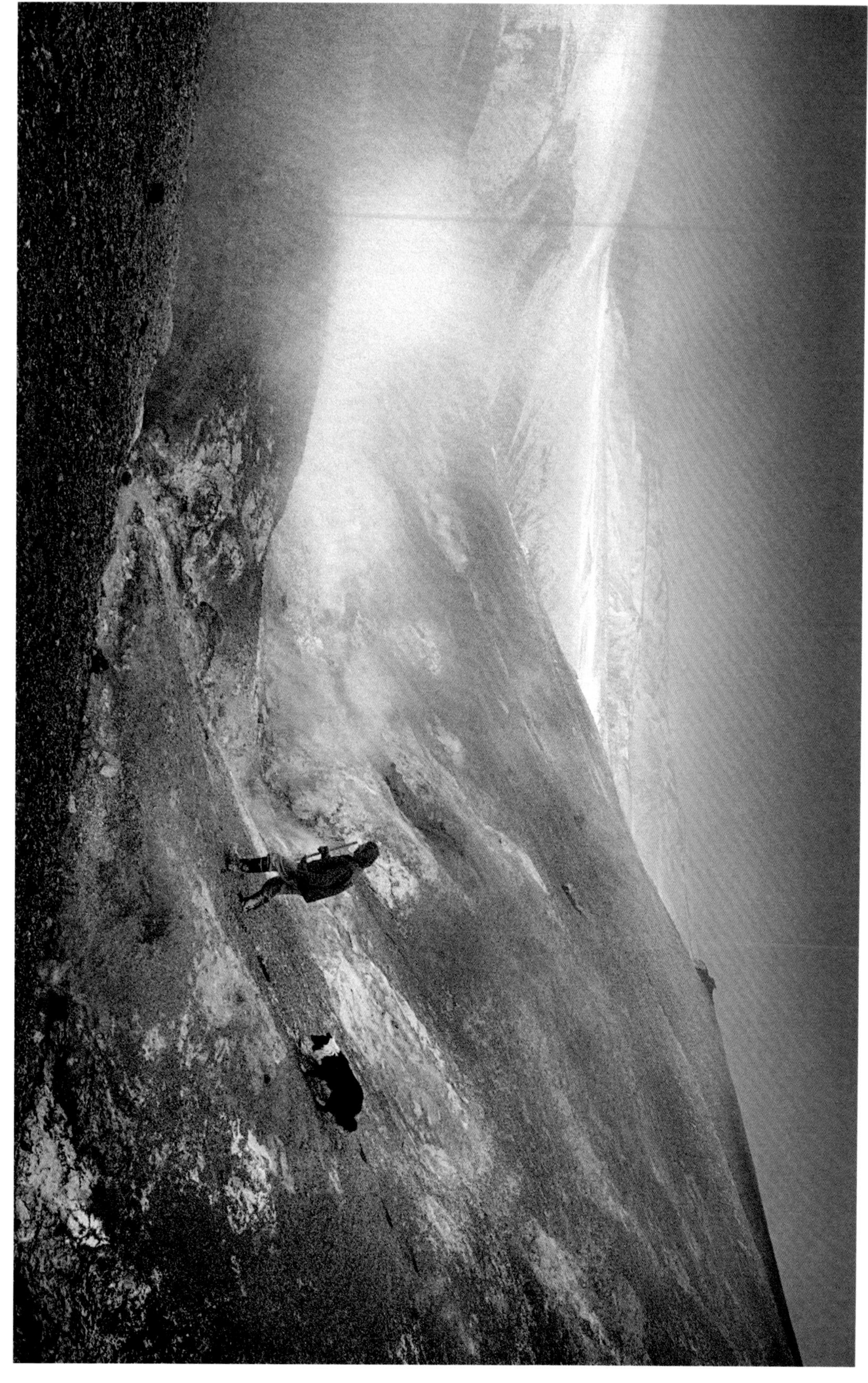

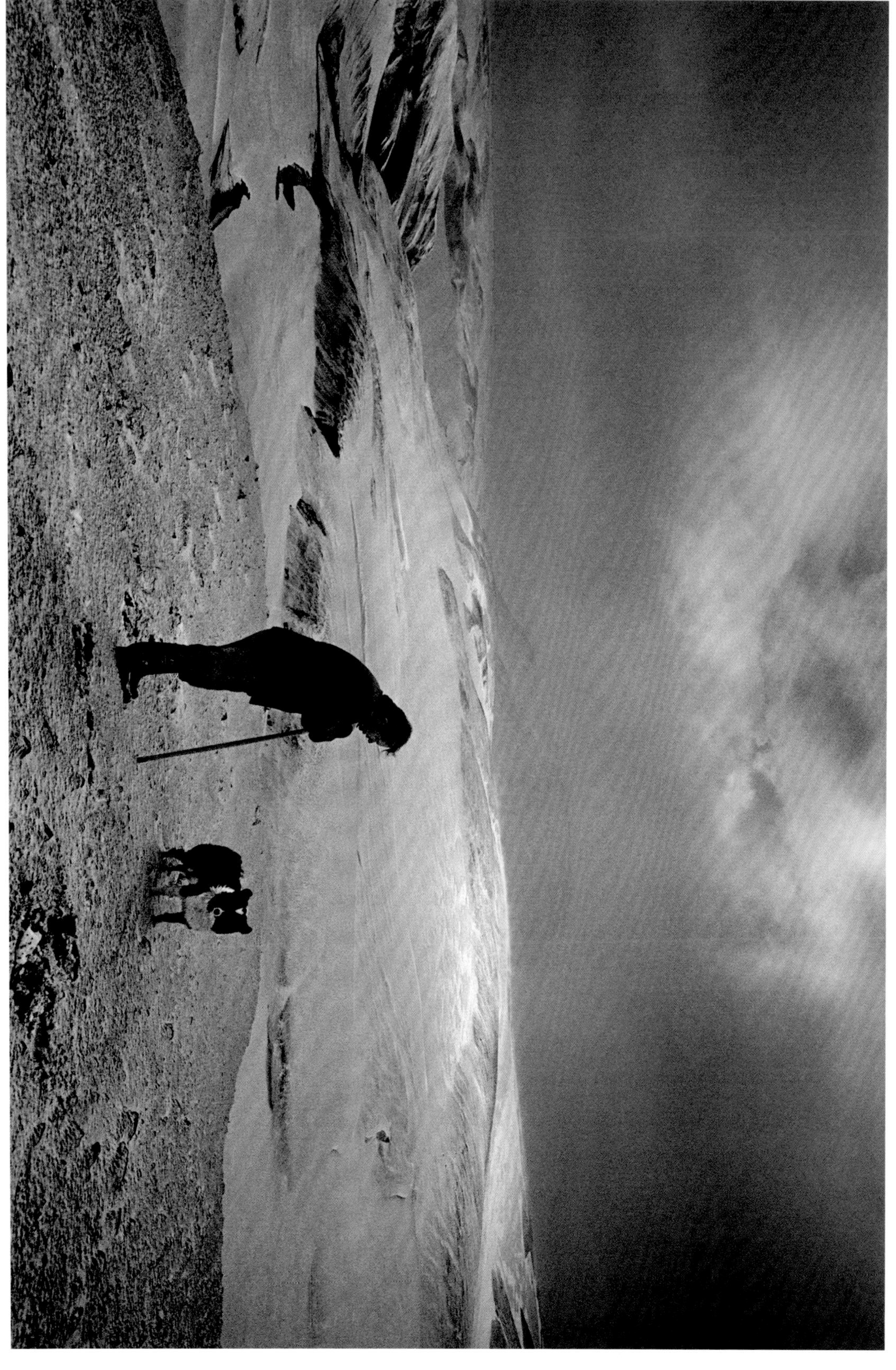

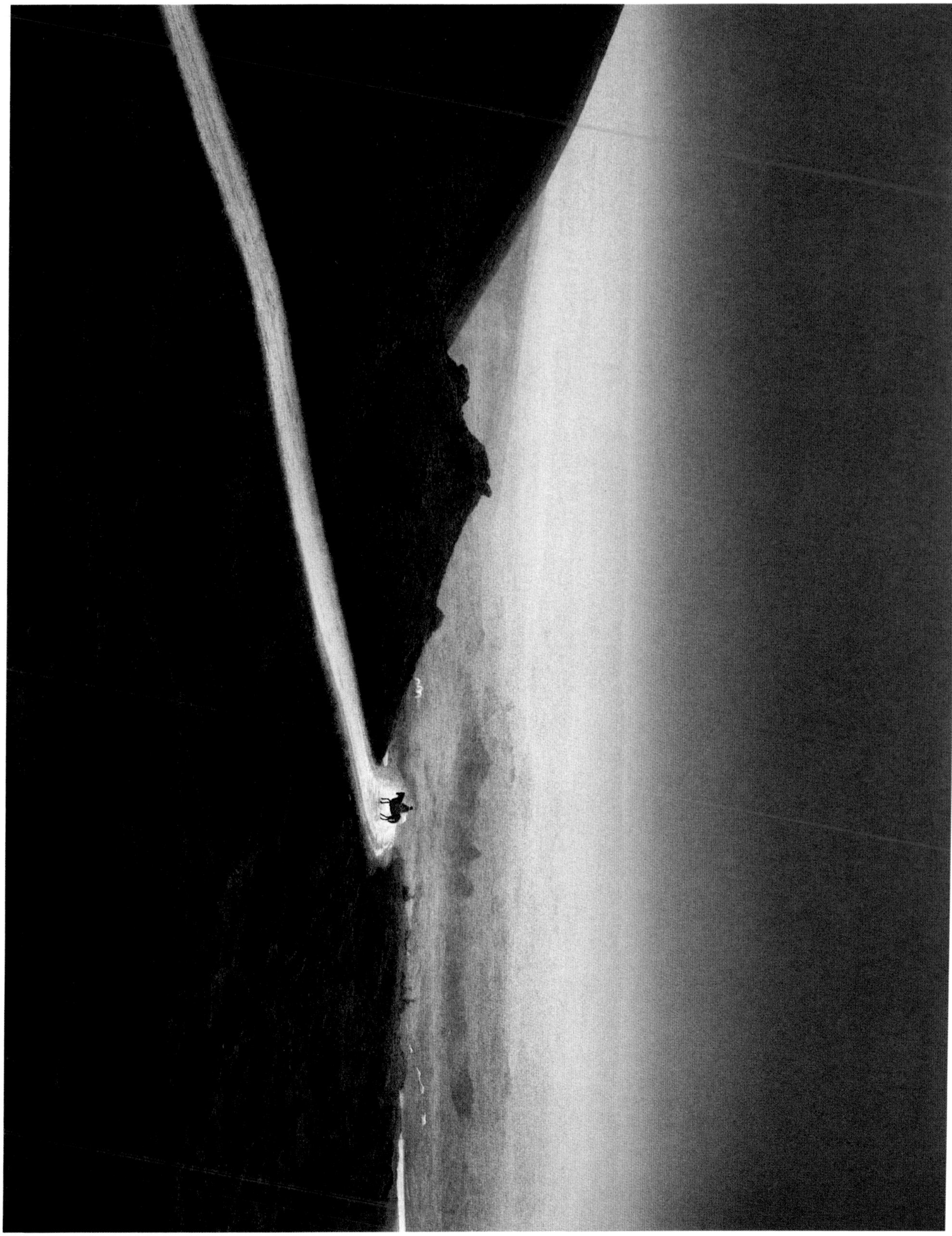

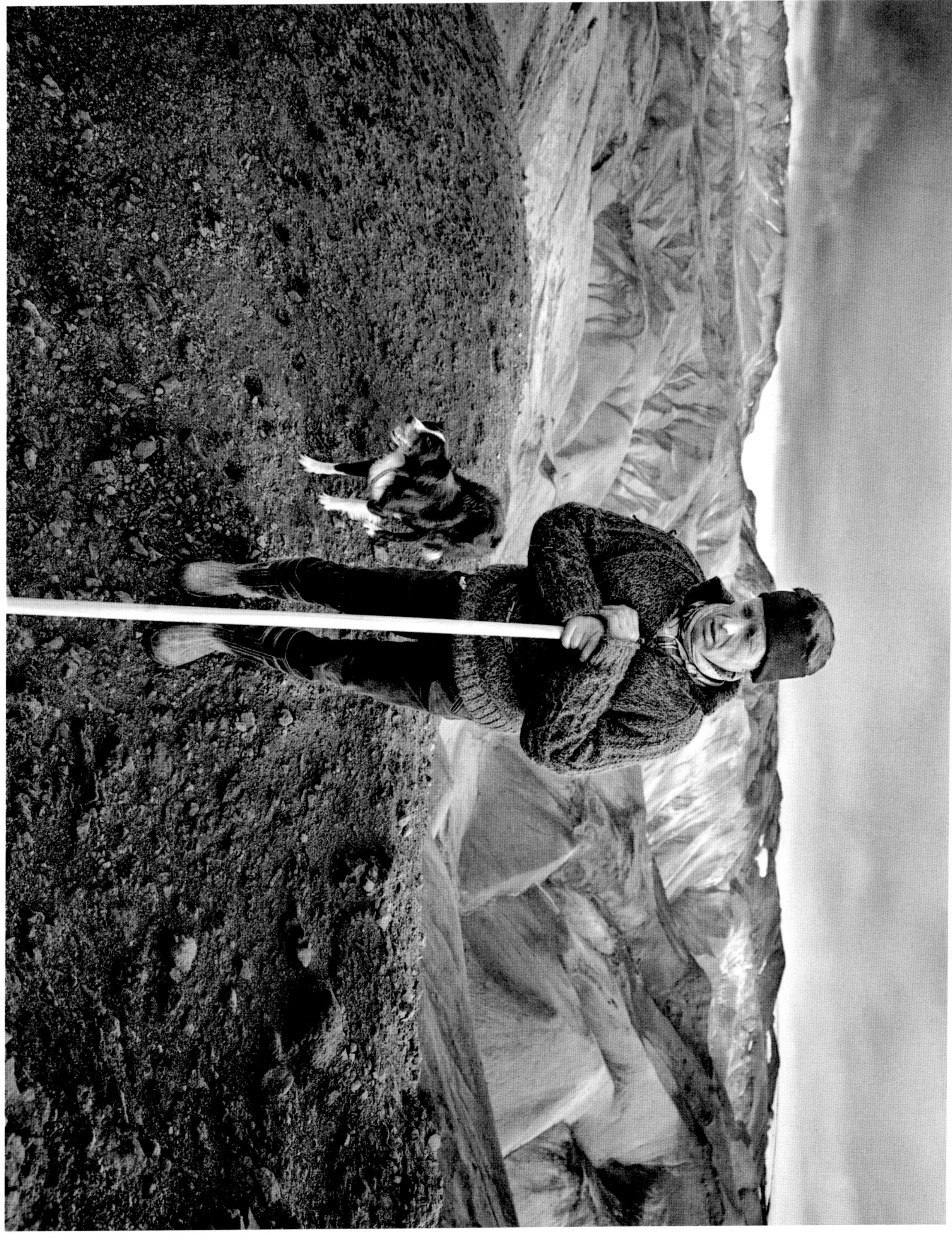

VI

Whiteout

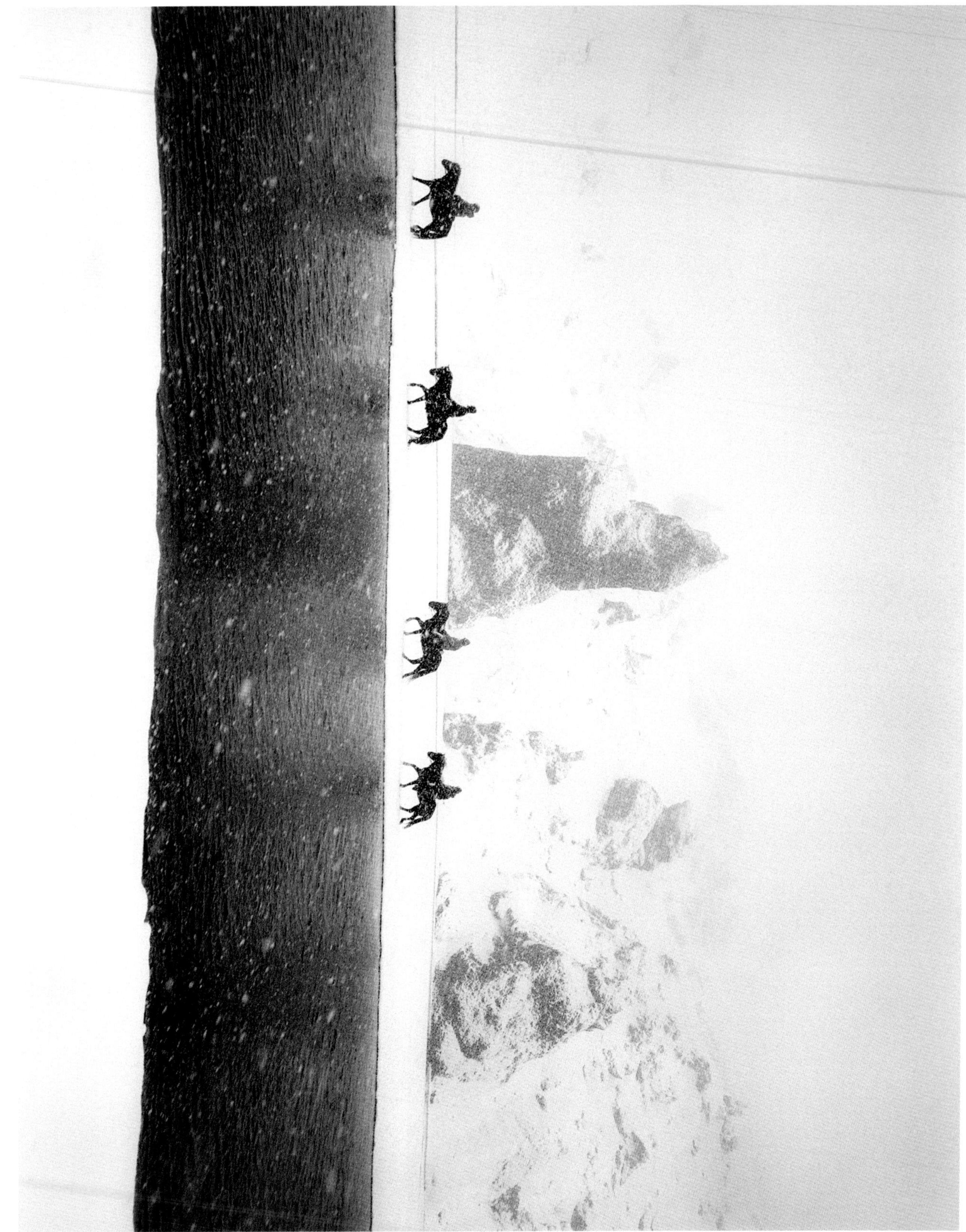

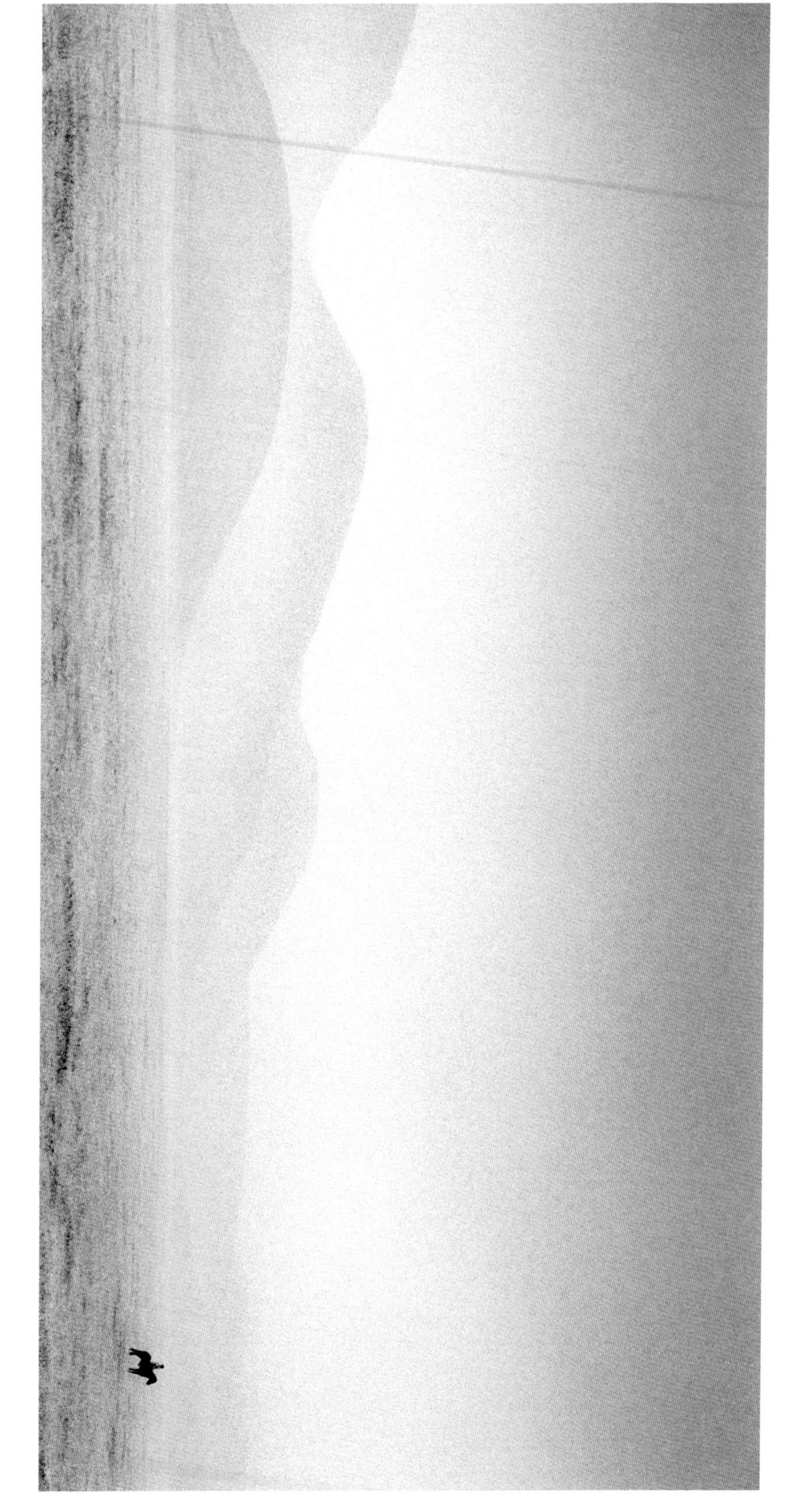

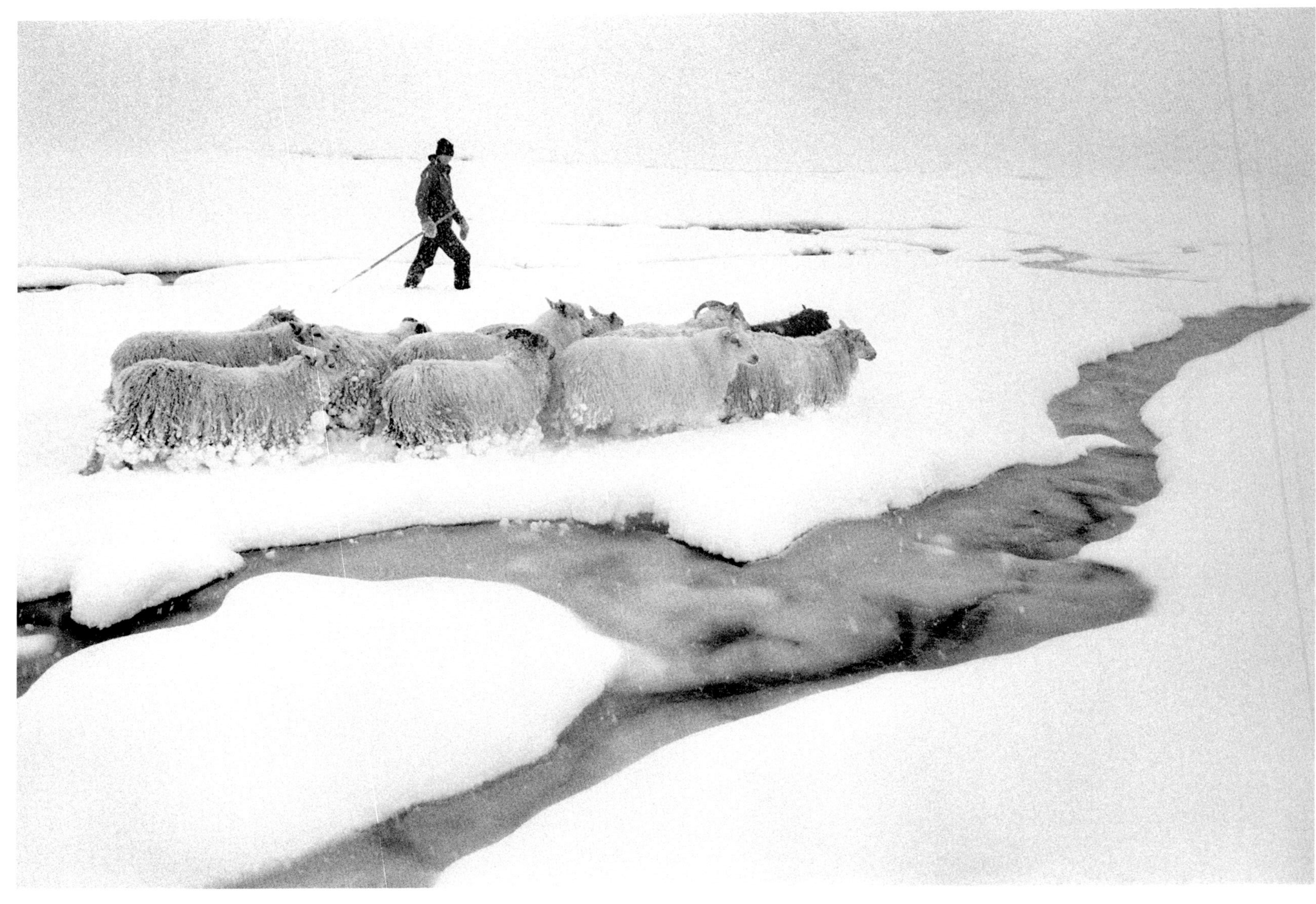

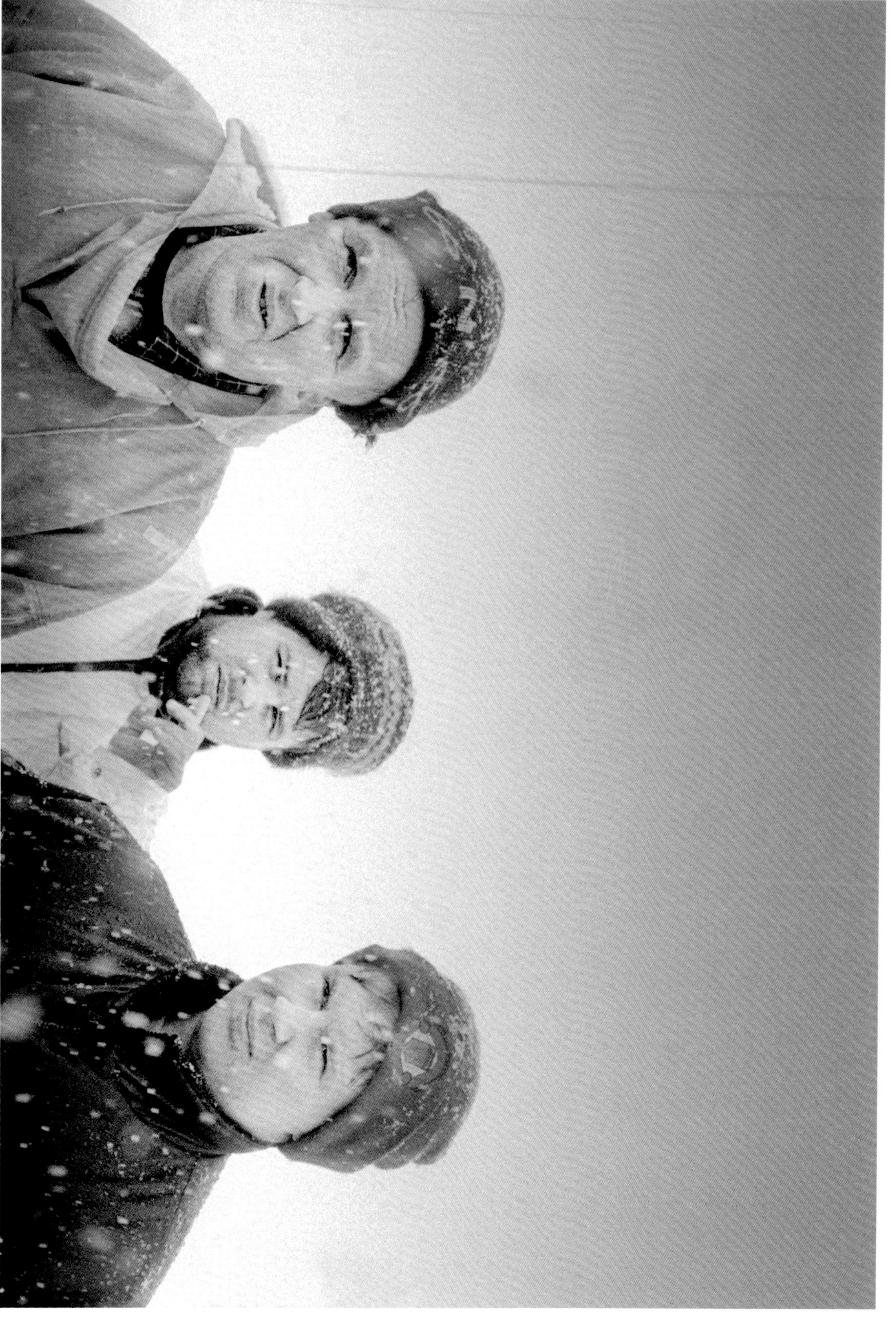

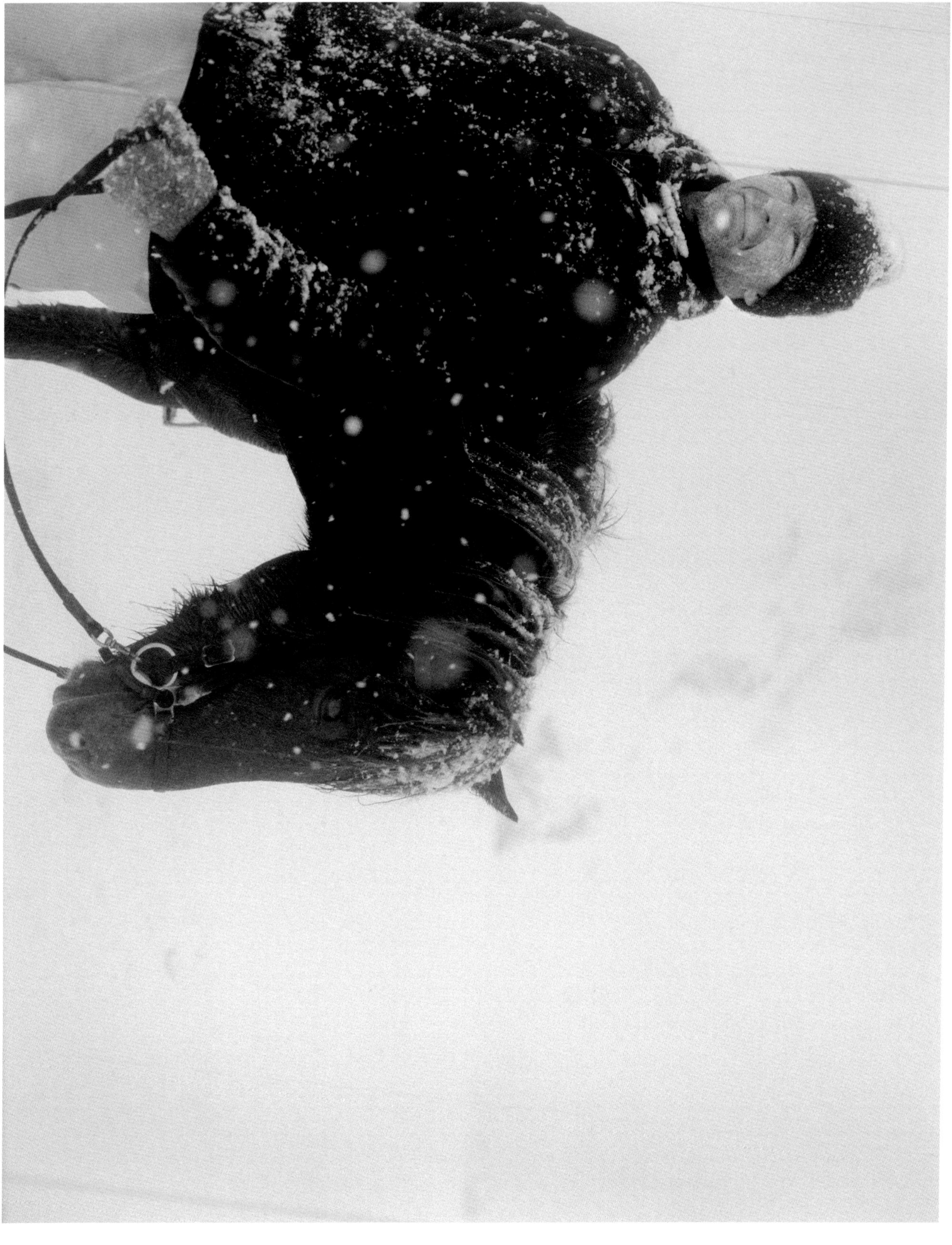

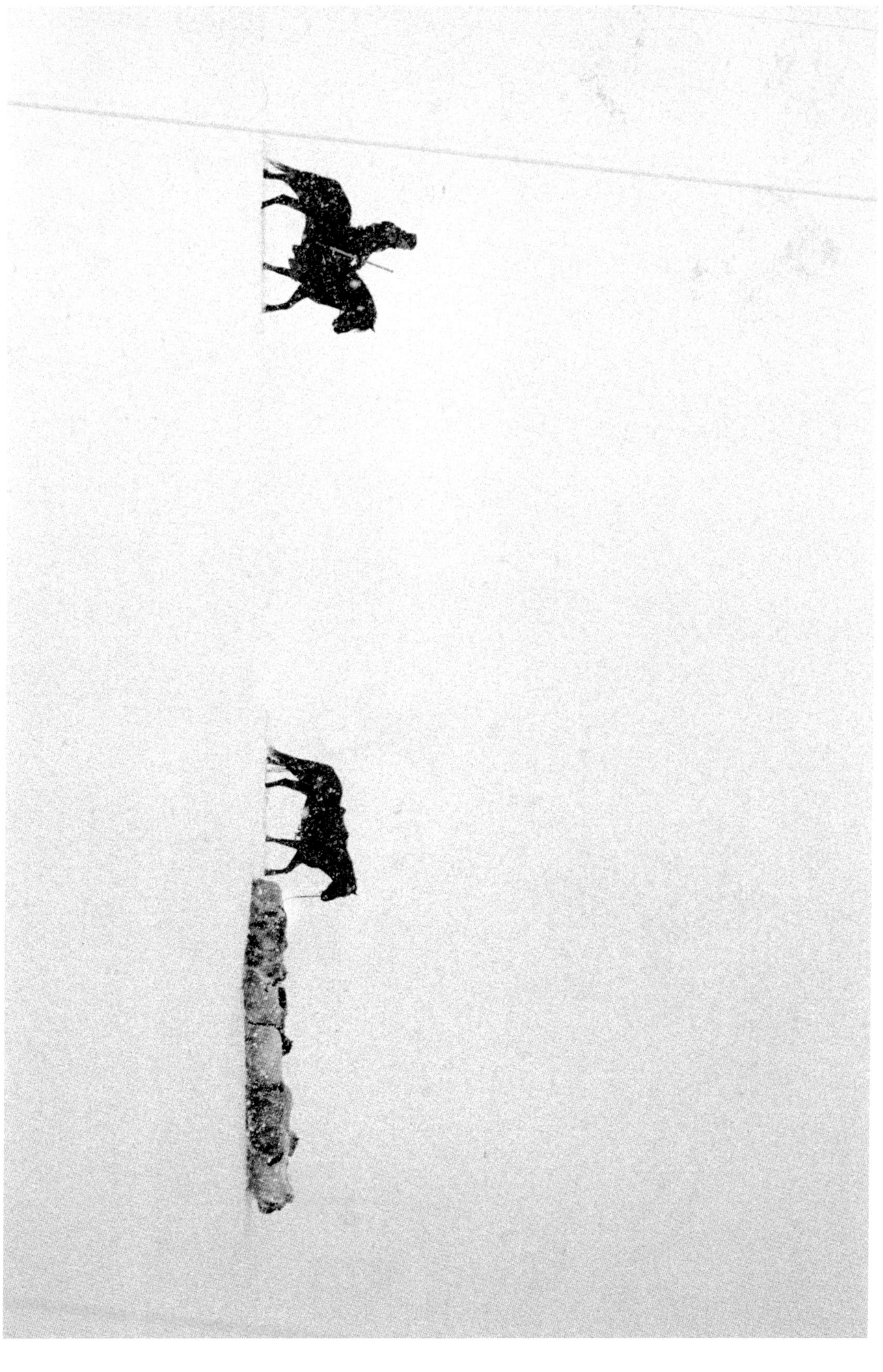

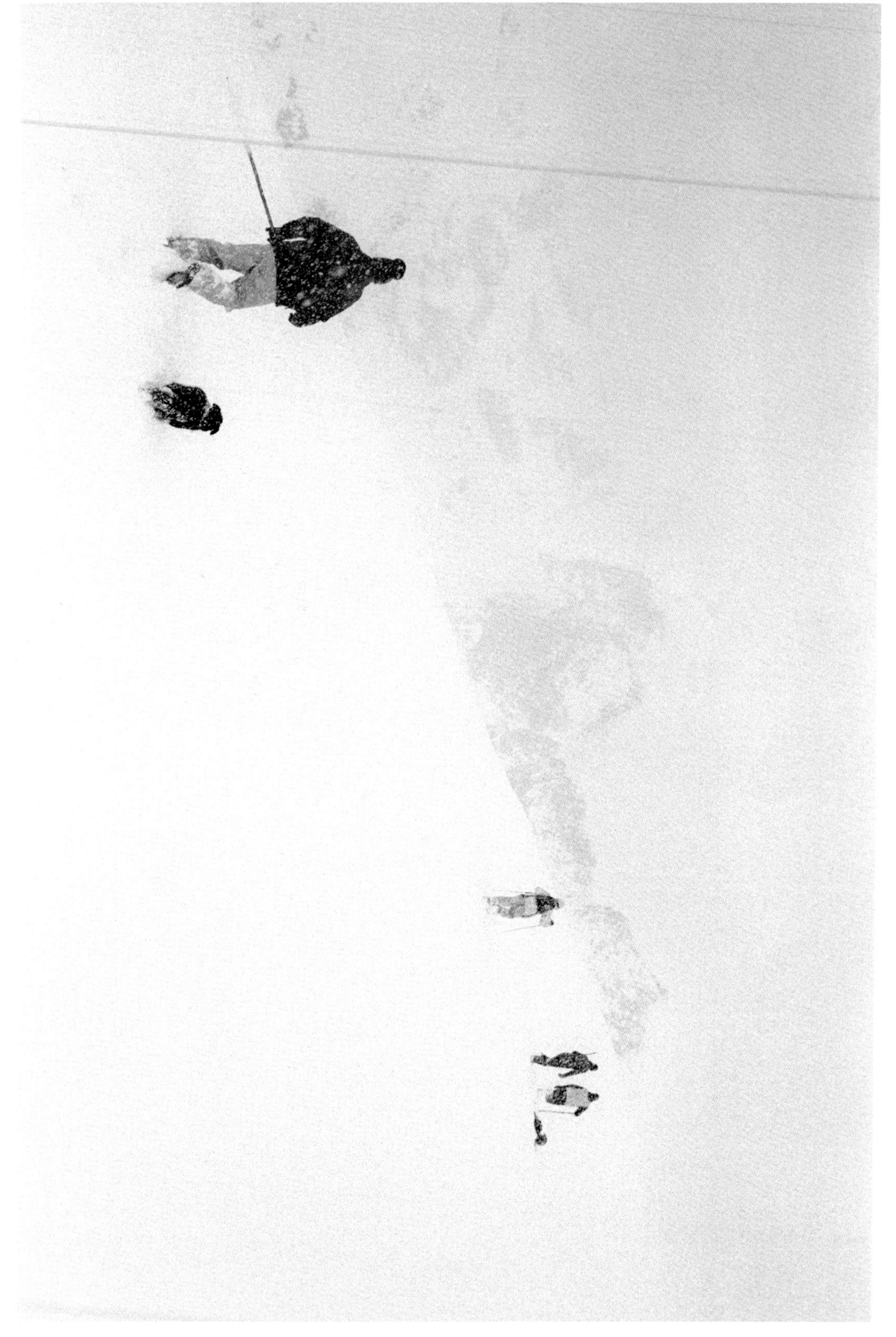

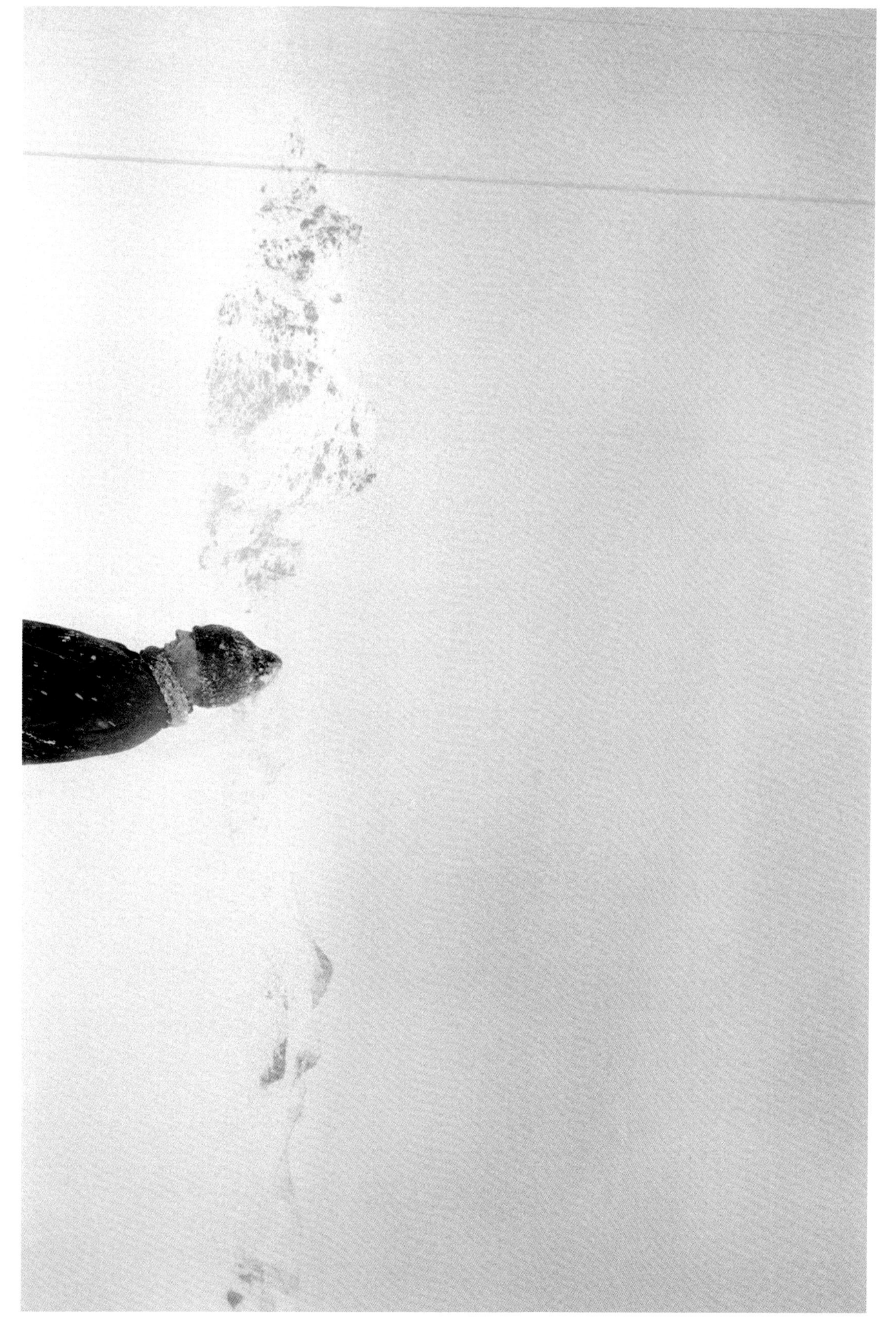

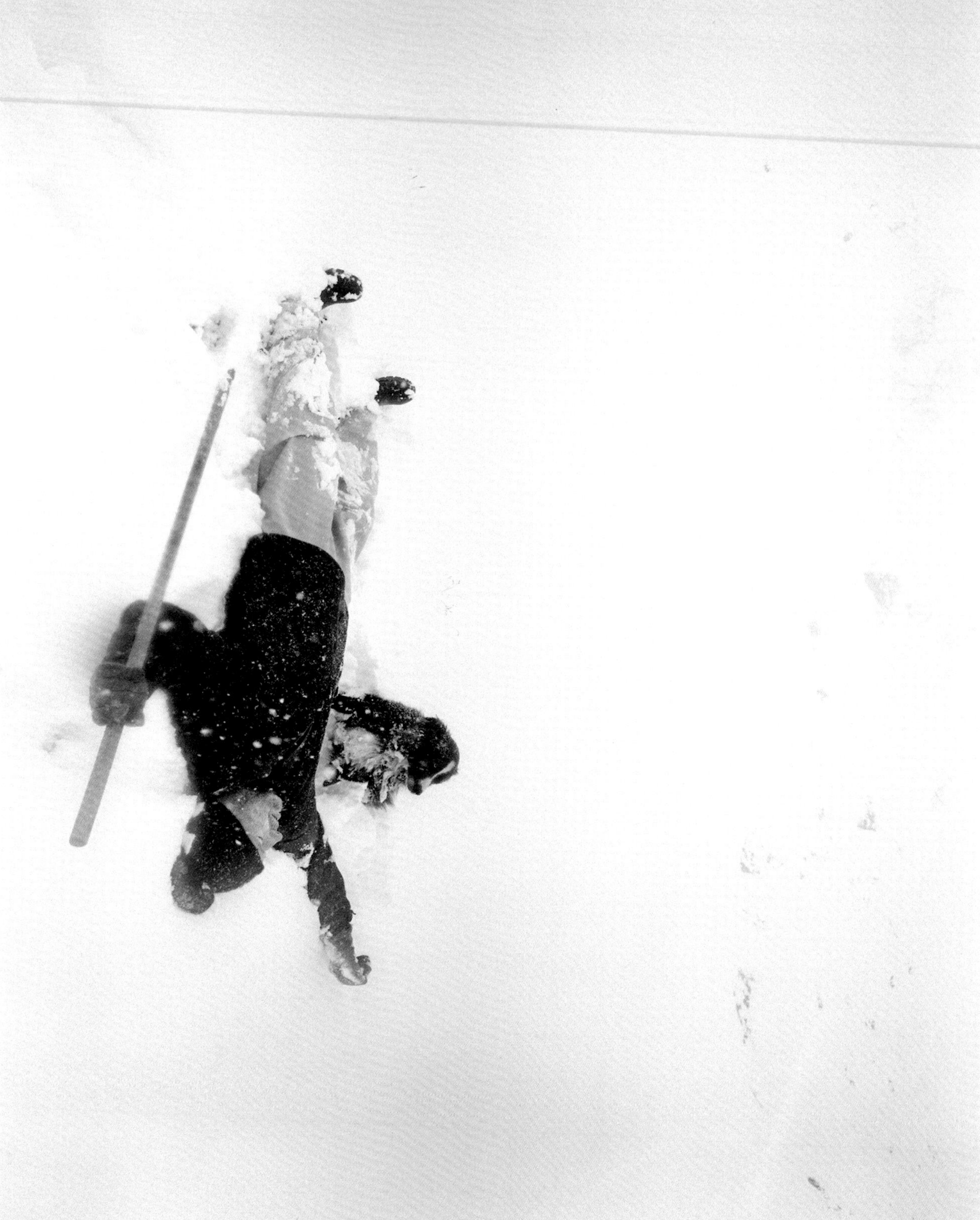

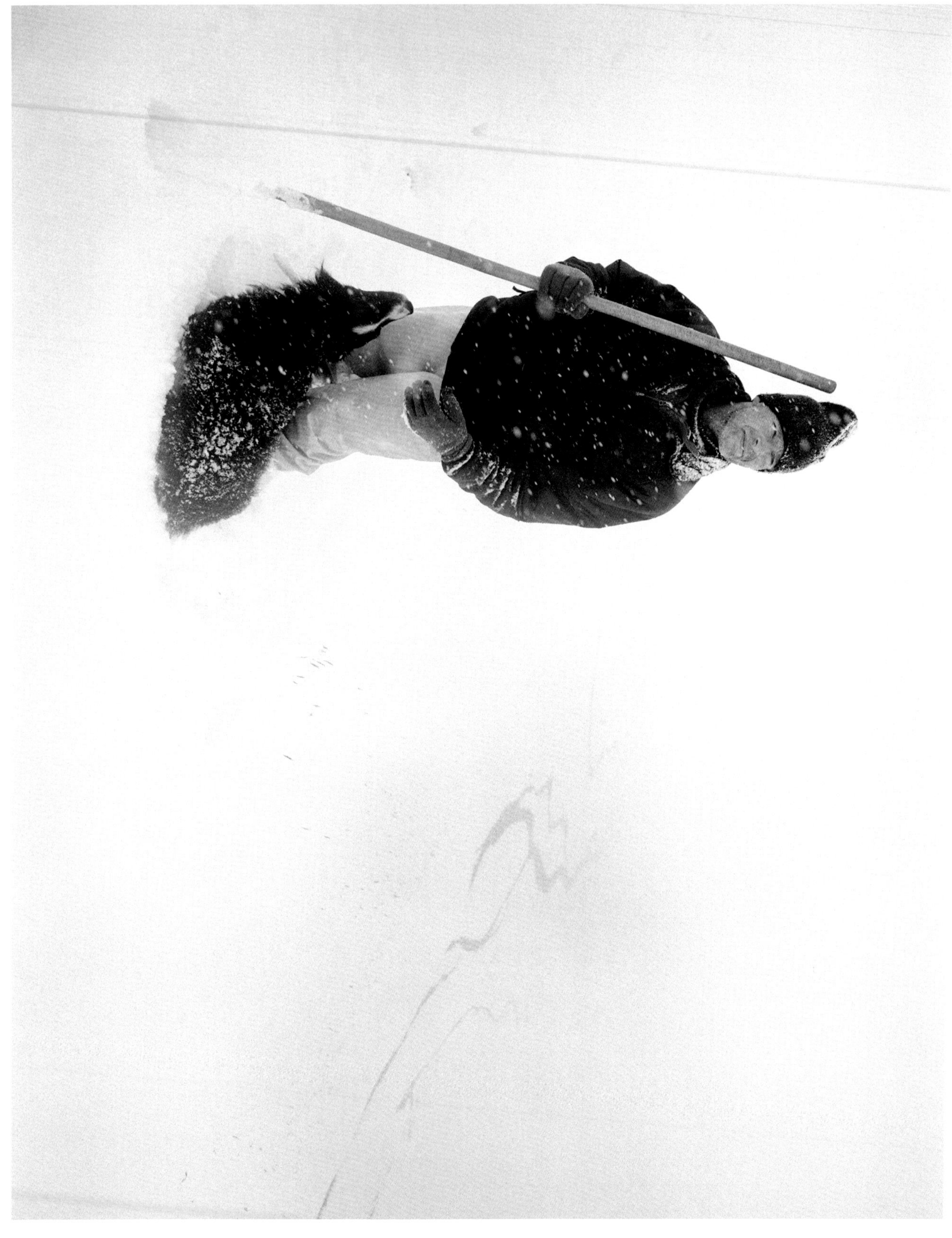

List of photographs

This book is dedicated to all the farmers of Landmannaafréttur, past and present. I thank those who took me with them into the mountains and allowed me to photograph them. I owe my greatest thanks to the mountain king, Kristinn from Skarð, and the storyteller, Þórður from Kaldakinn.

Ragnar Axelsson

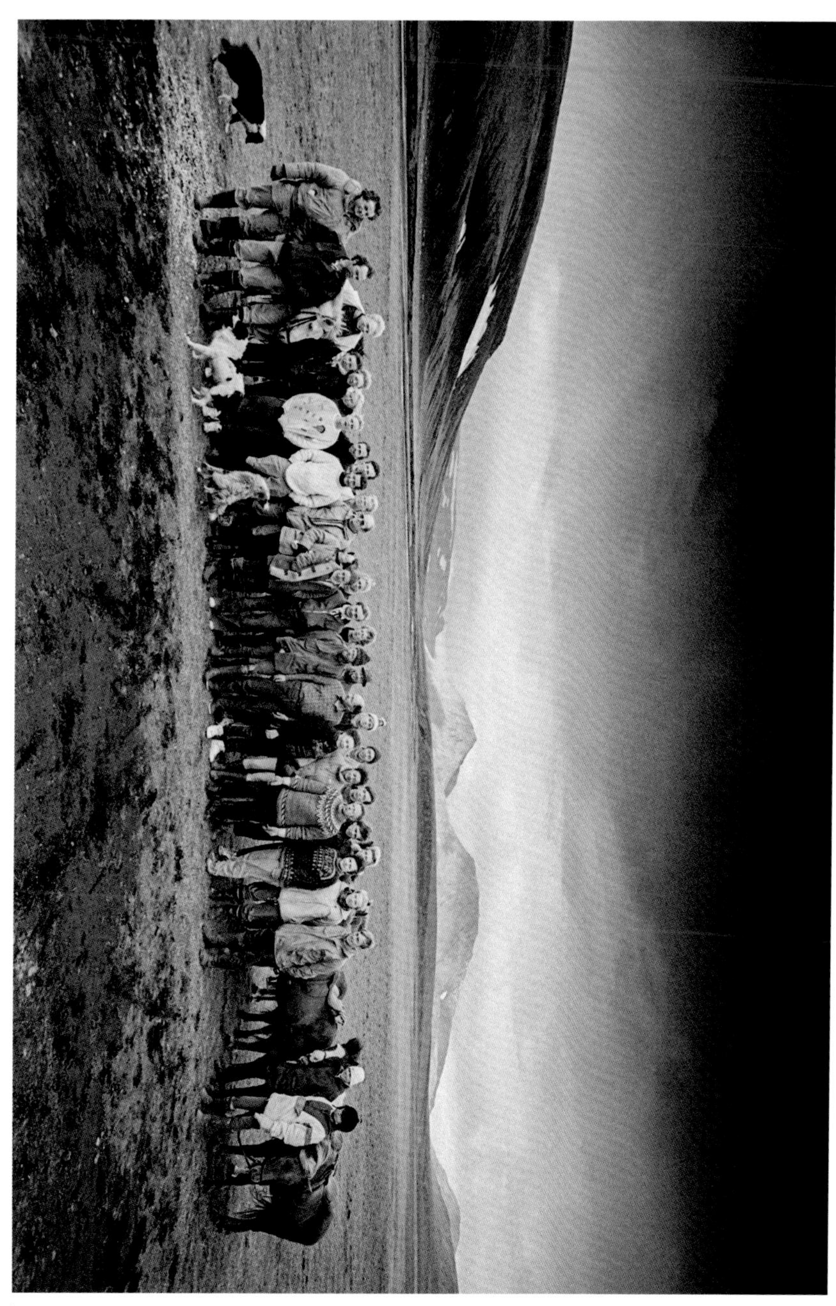

For over forty years, Ragnar Axelsson, known as Rax (b. 1958), has been photographing the people, animals, and landscape of the most remote regions of the Arctic, including Iceland, Siberia, and Greenland. In stark black-and-white images, he captures the elemental, human experience of nature at the edge of the liveable world, making visible the extraordinary relationships between the people of the Arctic and their extreme environment – relationships now being altered in profound and complex ways by unprecedented climate change.

A photojournalist at the Icelandic daily *Morgunblaðið* from 1976 to 2020, Ragnar has also worked on freelance assignments in Latvia, Lithuania, Mozambique, South Africa, China, and Ukraine. His photographs have been featured in *Life*, *Newsweek*, *Stern*, *Geo*, *National Geographic*, *Time*, and *Polka*, and have also been exhibited widely.

Ragnar has published eight books in various international editions. His most recent, *Arctic Heroes*, was published in 2020, and *Jökull/Glacier* was published in 2018, with a foreword by Ólafur Elíasson. *Andlit Nordursins/Faces of The North* was published in 2016, with a foreword by Mary Ellen Mark, and won the 2016 Icelandic Literary Prize for non-fiction. Other awards for Ragnar's work include numerous Icelandic photojournalist awards; the Leica Oskar Barnack Award (Honorable Mention); Grand Prize, Photo de Mer, Vannes; and Iceland's highest honour, the Order of the Falcon, Knight's Cross.

Ragnar is currently working on a three-year project documenting people's lives in all eight countries of the Arctic. At this pivotal time, as climate change irrevocably disrupts the physical and traditional realities of their world, Ragnar is bearing witness to the immediate and direct threat that changes in the climate pose to these people and their survival.

These pictures were taken in Landmannaafréttur and in the Landssveit region, Iceland, between 1980 and 2022.

www.rax.is

Design: Einar Geir Ingvarsson
Support: Haraldur Sigurðsson
Copy Editing: Philip Thomas

Project Management: Kehrer Verlag (Sylvia Ballhause)
Image Processing: Kehrer Design (René Henoch, Patrick Horn)
Production Management: Kehrer Design (Tom Streicher)

Bibliographic information published by
the Deutsche Nationalbibliothek
The Deutsche Nationalbibliothek lists this publication
in the Deutsche Nationalbibliografie; detailed bibliographic
data is available on the Internet at https://dnb.dnb.de.

Printed and bound in the EU
ISBN 978-3-96900-195-0

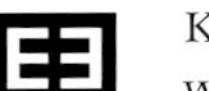
Kehrer Verlag Heidelberg
www.kehrerverlag.com